RICH IS NOT
A FOUR-LETTER
WORD

RICH IS NOT
A FOUR-LETTER
WORD

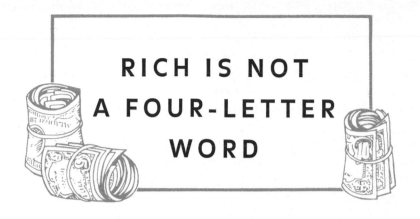

How to Survive Obamacare,
Trump Wall Street, Kick-Start Your Retirement,
and Achieve Financial Success

GERRI WILLIS

CROWN
FORUM
NEW YORK

Library of Congress Cataloging-in-Publication Data
Names: Willis, Gerri, author.
Title: Rich is not a four-letter word : how to survive
Obamacare, trump Wall Street, kick-start your retirement,
and achieve financial success / Gerri Willis.
Description: New York : Crown Forum, 2016.
Identifiers: LCCN 2015035325 | ISBN 9781101903797
Subjects: LCSH: Finance, Personal.
Classification: LCC HG179 .W535154 2016 | DDC 332.024—dc23
LC record available at http://lccn.loc.gov/2015035325

ISBN 978-1-101-90379-7
eBook ISBN 978-1-101-90380-3

Printed in the United States of America

Book design by Barbara Sturman
Jacket design by Tal Goretsky

1 3 5 7 9 10 8 6 4 2

First Edition

To my husband, David,
whose pan-roasted Sunday chicken
allowed this book to be written.
Of course, his incredible patience helped too.

CONTENTS

AUTHOR'S NOTE

I wrote this book for the many people who've never recovered from the Great Recession. The unemployed get much of the media's attention—and sympathy—but the unemployment rate tells only part of the story. Millions more of us struggle with other nasty problems that have come to define this sorry, no-growth economy. I'm thinking of the dads who may have found part-time work, but can't nail down a full-time gig with benefits. There are also the newly minted college grads living in basement apartments, shell-shocked that their massive investment in education has failed to pay off. Then, there're the retirees facing savings diminished by a decade's worth of Federal Reserve easy money policy. And, don't forget the families who thought Obamacare would protect them from the high cost of healthcare but now struggle to pay unaffordable premiums for coverage they are forced by the government to buy.

Yes, this recession has posed entirely new problems and created new stresses on our wallets. But Americans are a can-do lot. And when things go wrong, many of us take it on our own shoulders. We say *we* should have done better. *We* should have planned better. We blame ourselves. Many of those unemployed dads and struggling college grads think they somehow came up short. I don't believe that's true.

What's going on with our middle class today is different. Truth is, the heated rhetoric emanating from Washington, D.C., isn't helping you take care of your family and plan your future. Instead of helping, the liberal policies that have defined the last six years are flattening the middle class. As I write, the Social Security Administration has just issued a report revealing that more than half of Americans earn $30,000 or less a year. That's just $5,750 above the poverty line. That's a tragedy!

I believe it's time we do better. We must end the liberal, so-called "progressive" policies that are driving our middle class into extinction, and encourage the self-starters and entrepreneurs who can drive employment and growth. Wealth has been demonized by the Left in this country, but the reality is that financial success is necessary to raising up our children and their children. *Rich* is not a four-letter word. Moving ahead and moving up is something we've always been about. Financial success is a laudable goal!

If you want more for your family, this is a book worth picking up. I trace the roots of the problems for the middle class and offer solutions and shortcuts for people who want to make it on their own. Because I think you can still make it in this country under your own steam. The blame game is a waste of time and energy that can best be used on more productive pursuits.

How can I be so sure that your problems can be overcome? I've seen the struggle firsthand and witnessed it being overcome. As a coal miner's granddaughter, I witnessed my family in western North Carolina struggle with poverty and the shame that goes with it. Some had no indoor plumbing. Others received government handouts. But many, my father included, built successful lives that provided for their kin. It took grit and a willingness to try new things to succeed. But it proved to me that financial success *is* possible in this country even for those who must start from scratch. That's how I know you can achieve financial success, and I want to help you do it!

ACKNOWLEDGMENTS

This book would not have been possible without a very large group of people who assisted me and gave me advice along the way. My great thanks go to my Fox family, which has been so very supportive over the years. Thank you first and foremost to Roger Ailes, whose intelligence and strong leadership guide Fox News Channel and Fox Business Network every day. Thank you to Bill Shine, Gary Schreier, and Thomas Bowman, whose judgment and guidance I greatly appreciate. Thanks as well to Shepard Smith, Sean Hannity, Bill Hemmer, Martha MacCallum, and Greta Van Susteren for being so supportive. Show producers Kim Rosenberg, Alan Komissaroff, Kevin Burke, Jessica Tomidy, and Brad Hirst have been unbelievably generous.

Writing *Rich Is Not a Four-Letter Word* has been

invigorating and a pleasure, but it wouldn't have been possible without the top-notch team at Penguin Random House's Crown Publishing Group. Great thanks to Crown executive editor Roger Scholl, and to Crown's incredible marketing and publicity team: Campbell Wharton, Ayelet Gruenspecht, and Megan Perritt. Thanks as well to my agent, Wayne Kabak, who was a critical sounding board.

There were also a number of people whose expertise I leaned on heavily to create the tools, tips, and advice I hope will help many Americans. Those people include, but are not limited to, David Bach, Tony Beshara, Kal Chany, Ric Edelman, Lauren Fix, Rob Franek, Vera Gibbons, Scott Gottlieb, Scott Hodge, Doug Holtz-Eakin, Paul Howard, Tom Kraeutler, Adam Levin, Greg McBride, Grover Norquist, and Pete Sepp.

My family has also been an unwavering source of support. Thanks to my mother, Betty Jean Conley; sister, Frankie Pryor; and brother, Steve Willis. There is one person, though, who is behind me every day, giving me the benefit of his intelligence, wit, and humor, and that's my husband of 21 years, David Evans. Nobody compares. Thank you, David!

RICH IS NOT
A FOUR-LETTER
WORD

1

IT'S NOT YOUR FAULT
YOU'RE NOT RICH

We've lost it. Our mojo. Our critical faith in things. Our confidence. The vast majority of Americans—85 percent—say it is now more difficult to maintain their standard of living than it was in 2002. That's 10 long years of frustration for a country accustomed to regular and consistent improvements in its way of life. In the same survey, 43 percent of us say it's never getting better. It's no wonder people are discouraged. Median wages have declined sharply since 2006 and are lower still than the $54,059 registered in President Barack Obama's first year in office (as of July 2015). Worrisome enough for sure, but the statistics that really shocked me were contained in a 2014 Pew Research Center study that showed that fewer and fewer of us think of ourselves as middle class. Since 2008, the proportion of Americans who identify themselves as mainstream has fallen by nearly a fifth from 53 percent to just 44 percent. Forty percent of us now identify ourselves as lower middle class or lower class compared with only 25 percent in February 2008. We're defining *ourselves* down. What happened to American middle-class confidence?

Most of us blame the Great Recession for this mess. We were on a roll before the deepest recession since World War II came crashing down. Remember? The stock market was going up, up, up, and so were housing prices. We felt rich! Home equity lines of credit bankrolled vacations, home improvements, literally anything we could imagine. Those were the days! By the time Lehman Brothers closed its doors and filed for bankruptcy on September 15, 2008, we had grown so used to the good times that we couldn't imagine the years of financial deprivation to come. But they did come, and many Americans gave back more than they had gained. Record foreclosures. Personal bankruptcies. Smashed retirement accounts. The anxiety and frustration caused by the Great Recession has been off the charts.

But those bad times, my friend, have all but ended. After 2008, the stock market rocketed higher for six straight years, creating the largest bull market of the last 24 years. The economy has been expanding for six years. So why, then, are Americans still depressed and on the sidelines? Why are we biding our time? I've covered Americans and their wallets for the better part of 25 years, and I can tell you I've never seen consumers in such a funk. Market pros tell me they are shocked that small investors haven't gotten back into the market in a bigger way. The last time the market performed so poorly was during the tech boom of the late 1990s, when day traders moved the markets as investing became a national pastime. Individual investors compared brokerage fees and results and swapped stock buying tips. Not this time. Today, only 14 percent of us own individual stocks, according to the Federal Reserve. Also confounding is just how stingy consumers have become at the local mall. Instead of jumping at a sale, shoppers sit back and wait for the next discount and the next. Christmas 2014 was the first time in memory that holiday sales declined in December from the previous month. What is keeping us down? The real problem in my view isn't the lingering effects of the last recession or even an aging boomer generation anxious about making a financial misstep before retirement. Don't blame the 1 percent either or corporate chieftains stashing cash overseas. The real culprit is right here at home.

If you're feeling poorer, less hopeful about your financial prospects, and worried about the future, you can blame the liberal progressive policies of President Barack Obama and his liberal allies. The progressive mind-set championed by the president allows bureaucrats to decide what's best for individuals, and that has meant more government, more bureaucracy, and more taxpayer money. The stimulus program, expanded welfare, and housing and education loan programs were designed to help Americans. Instead, these programs have burdened us with debt. Many have failed on their own terms. Obamacare, for example, has missed its mark. Originally intending to help 40 million people get healthcare coverage, government insurance policies have been accessed by just 10 million while damaging popular programs such as Medicare Advantage and raising health costs for the rest of us. Obama's promises about the program were broken over and over. It turns out you can't keep your doctor or your insurance policy. "Bending the cost curve" ended up meaning *you* pay for more. Even the most widely accepted government programs, such as federal college loans, have rebounded negatively under this administration as families have been buried under a mountain of student loan debt. These misguided efforts have come at the expense of middle-class America, which is presumed by this administration to have the resilience and the deep pockets to pay for anything. It does not. This chapter will examine how Obama's liberal progressive policies have set back middle-class Americans and threaten their financial future, but the balance of this book will be dedicated to finding solutions to the roadblocks to success put in place by liberal policies. You'll learn how those policies have fundamentally changed businesses, higher education, and healthcare systems as well as how to respond to those changes. I want you to succeed and be financially successful on your own terms.

My mother used to say you can afford anything if the price is right, but the sad truth is that we can't afford the president's policies. Under Obama's watch, the national debt has spiraled $6 trillion to $18 trillion. No other president has seen the national tab rise to such a level. It was under Obama's watch that credit rating agencies downgraded the government's pristine AAA credit rating, making our debt even more expensive. Were the federal debt to be paid by each and every American, the tab would be $57,000 per capita. But let's face it, only *taxpayers* actually bear the burden. Broken down in that way, the tab is $154,000 per taxpayer, a debt that is likely to persist for generations. Already government forecasts call for federal deficits to hit $21 trillion by 2124. Liberals have promoted this debt as the only way to rebound from recession, but federal spending didn't evaporate with the recession; instead it continued to grow, creating an ever larger tab to be paid down the road. Regardless of what liberal progressive economists say, that bill will come due. As any small-business operator knows, you can't live on credit forever. In the meantime, however, the president's policies have stung Americans in a more immediately painful way.

Obama's antibusiness rhetoric and punishing regulatory agenda have led U.S. corporations to take their foot off the expansion pedal, keeping their cash on the balance sheet as they warily watch for the next burdensome rule to come down the pike from Washington. For example, after President Obama announced that he wanted to regulate the Internet, AT&T stopped spending money on developing Internet services. Millions upon millions of dollars of investment were suspended that could have employed Americans. The same story is true of many other industries. The president's war on coal has killed tens of thousands of jobs. Small banks have downsized or even gone out of business altogether under the repressive rules of Dodd-Frank that were supposed to reign in the biggest banks but ended up hamstringing community lenders.

Liberals seem to regard private sector initiative as economic kudzu, something that can never be stamped out and therefore can be tinkered with endlessly. But they are wrong. Because of these progressive policies the usual expansion and hiring that accompany recovery have been painfully slow to develop. There's been little relief from small-business expansion either. The nation's largest employer, small business, has put growth on hold as Obamacare has penalized small businesses with payrolls topping 50 or more with a $2,000 tax per employee if they don't offer healthcare coverage.

Why does this antibusiness policy pushed by Obama matter so much to middle-class Americans? Economic growth is essential to the American economy and American families. A change of a single percentage point in growth can spell the difference between an economy that creates more and better jobs and one that barely sputters along. More growth means higher pay, bonuses, and more job opportunities. But when growth flatlines to 1.5 percent as it did in the seven years after 2007, families are less likely to buy a home, send their kids to college, or buy an extra car. The U.S.

economy's long-term growth rate of 3 percent has been the envy of the developed world. If growth had averaged something closer to that level in Obama's first six years, the economy would have created another 1.2 million jobs. If growth had risen to 3.5 percent, another 2.5 million jobs would have been created. It's simple. The more expansion we have, the better the jobs market gets, and the higher incomes become as well. Faster growth allowed Americans to double their incomes in the 40 years between 1947 and 1987, jumping from $30,000 to $69,000 (in constant 2012 dollars). If their kids had experienced another 26 years of typical growth, their incomes by 2013 would have been $118,000 *on average*. Of course, that didn't happen.

Having suffered through six years of liberal progressive policies, working Americans' wallets are lighter. According to the American Action Forum's Doug Holtz-Eakin, an economist who once ran the Congressional Budget Office, 3.0 percent economic growth for those who've been waiting in vain for a raise would mean another $4,200 in average incomes, and 3.5 percent would boost income growth an additional $4,500 to $9,000. That's money left on the table because our economy couldn't get past stall speed and this administration's aggressive liberal policies shocked American business into inaction. We've hobbled along. Sixty percent of the jobs lost during the Great Recession were middle-income occupations. In the years immediately after the recession, 73 percent of the jobs added were low income in sectors such as hospitality, restaurants, and retail. That's a poor exchange for workers. As late as June 2015, three out of five Americans told pollsters that the economy was still in recession six years *into the recovery.*

Our experience simply doesn't square with what we're used to. Most of us have taken it for granted that the American economy will always expand. We believed that with the exception of the occasional recession, the American way of life, an expanding economic base, and better opportunities could continue forever. I remember my older sister telling me as a young woman that she could never fall out of the middle class because she had been born into it. She believed, as many people did, that the American economy is like the Grand Canyon, a naturally occurring feature that can go on and on. That's why I believe Americans are still distrustful and depressed about this economy. They know that something has changed fundamentally—and for the worse.

As late as 2014, nearly one in four Americans of working age was jobless. Labor force participation, the flip side of unemployment, plummeted to levels not seen since women started entering the workforce en masse 40 years ago. Three-quarters of us either have lost a job or have a relative or close friend who has in the last few years. We ask ourselves, What is going on? What has happened to our country? Why are opportunities so scarce? This is epic, game-changing stuff regardless of the frequent posturing by the Obama administration.

For progressives, the enemy that has turned their policies into economic failures is the wealthy 1 percent. Over and over, the president has called out the superwealthy. It's true they've done very well over the six years of the president's tenure, but they aren't the authors of this anemic recovery. Obama would have you believe that the gains of the 1 percent have come at the expense of the 99 percent. But that's not true. It's not how capitalism works. There is no one pot of money all of us must take from. The reason capitalist economies have been so successful is that they are dynamic. In short, they expand and all participants can expand with them.

The hard reality for progressive liberals is that although they were handed a recovery five months into Obama's first administration, they have failed to capitalize on it for the American people. Their legacy is towering federal debt, poor job prospects, and anemic economic growth. It is those realities which are sapping the confidence of Americans. The once-indestructible self-assuredness of the American people is no more, and that is reflected in the lack of confidence we have in providing for ourselves and making our own way. My goal in *Rich Is Not a Four-Letter Word* is to reinvigorate that confidence and show how it is still possible, even with a fundamentally altered playing field, to make it and prosper. Together, we are going to get your mojo back.

I'll start by showing you exactly how Obama's policies are harming your bottom line. You'll see examples of waste and abuse of your tax dollars, incompetence, and poor policy making that targets Americans' wallets.

HOW WE GOT OFF TRACK

To understand how liberal progressive policies have undermined American wealth, let's go back to the beginning. President Obama's first legislative initiative, the stimulus act, was passed by Congress on February 17, 2009, less than a month after the president's inauguration. It was the biggest economic recovery package in the nation's history, originally $787 billion in stimulus spending (it would blossom to $830 billion later) that was supposed to pull us out of the Great Recession. Instead, it turned into a hopelessly mismanaged giveaway that failed in its fundamental objective: bailing the economy out of the biggest downturn since the Great Depression. The idea was to use government spending to create economic demand where none exists. That idea came from John Maynard Keynes, a British economist of the early twentieth century who believed that recessions should be fought with taxpayer dollars. In fact, according to his theory, it didn't matter much what the government was buying. What mattered was that government was spending, and spending big. Imagine workers being paid to dig a hole and then refill that hole. Over and over. Workers get paid, so goes the Keynesian argument, and then spend that money in the economy, which creates demand for grocery store own-ers, butchers, and the like. Economic activity is supposed to bubble up like a pot of water boiling on the stove with the government providing the burner. But that didn't happen for two reasons. First, the money didn't reach its destination; much of it was wasted. Second, Americans who did receive stimulus dollars didn't react in the way Keynes anticipated. They didn't spend; they saved.

Despite the president's promise that stimulus dol-lars would "help those hardest hit by our economic crisis," *ProPublica*, a left of center nonprofit journal, reported that spending was not correlated with need. Stimulus dollars didn't go to the poorest parts of the country or even the places where joblessness was the most concentrated. The emphasis was getting the money out the door quickly. Echoing Keynes, Vice President Joe Biden called on local politicians to spend on "stupid things." And that is what happened. Much of the stimulus money went to the government and education sec-tors, where unemployment was low, but only 10 percent went to infrastructure, though unemployment in construction was running in double digits.

Then there was the out-and-out waste. Former Senator Tom Coburn, a famed tracker of wasted government dollars, issued a report 18 months after the bill was signed, detail-ing 100 projects in which taxpayer dollars were squandered. There was half a million dollars for new windows at the Mount St. Helens visitors center in Amboy, Washington.

The building had been closed since 2007, and there were no immediate plans to reopen it. Nearly $7 million went for repairs to an 1846 brick fort at the end of the Florida Keys even though few people could visit the remote national park unless they hired a seaplane or took a four-hour round-trip boat ride. Money also went to research projects: $2 million to send researchers from the California Academy of Sciences to islands in the Indian Ocean to study exotic ants, $296,000 for a study of dog domestication at Cornell University, and $141,000 to send students from Montana State University to China to study dinosaur eggs.

The fact that spending didn't target need didn't happen simply because government bean counters were ineffective or incompetent. There was a method to the spending stimulus madness, according to research by John Lott, a research scientist at the University of Maryland. Instead of states with high bankruptcy, foreclosure, and unemployment rates, Lott wrote, states with powerful Democratic representatives or ones that had voted for Obama in the presidential election got more money. States that had entirely Democratic congressional delegations received $460 more in stimulus dollars per person than did states that did not. The states in which Obama won by the largest margin in 2008 got the most money. Lower-income states got less. States with higher bankruptcy rates got less. States with high employment got less. Lott called the stimulus program a massive wealth transfer, but it was also doomed from the beginning because the money went to political cronies rather than to the people who needed it. Stimulus spending in other words was a waste.

As a result of this mismanagement, anniversaries of the stimulus spending bill came and went and still the president had little to show for the unprecedented outlay of taxpayer money. Five years after President Obama signed the American Recovery and Reinvestment Act the economy was still in dire straits. He said the spending would mark "the beginning of the end" of the nation's economic troubles. When the stimulus was passed the goal was to get unemployment to 5 percent. Six years later that goal was achieved, but only because millions of Americans dropped out of the workforce and others accepted part-time work.

Even the part of the stimulus that went directly to Americans didn't provide a Keynesian push to the economy. Even though payroll tax reductions put money immediately in people's hands, most saved that money rather than spending it. Stanford economist John Taylor theorized that this occurred because the tax cuts were temporary, not permanent. States used the money to pay down deficits or to save for a rainy day even though the expectation was that they would spend the money on new equipment and capital purchases that could goose the economy.

The president tried to rewrite his stimulus history again and again. On the campaign trail in early January 2015, he laid the groundwork for a State of the Union address later that month in which he would argue that his policies, particularly the stimulus spending, had turned the U.S. economy around. His first trip was to a Ford plant in Wayne, Michigan, a suburb of Detroit, where he said that the $80 billion infusion of taxpayer money into automakers in 2009 had rescued the industry. "There is no doubt that thanks to the steps that we took early on to rescue our economy we are entering into the New Year with a new confidence that America is coming back," the president said. True enough, the industry had enjoyed impressive sales the previous year, but it wasn't due to the bailout. The recovery in auto sales happened because of building demand among Americans who had held on to their cars for an average of 11 years, an all-time high. The economy recovered because of real need for products rather than a government program. Moreover, Ford was the one American automotive company that turned down the TARP (Troubled Asset Relief Program) money. Ford, under Alan Mulally, turned around Ford.

Even so, the president soldiered on, claiming his policies were successful. But the pictures told a different story. The Ford plant the president chose to speak from was closed because of lack of demand for the compact hybrid cars made there. About 5,000 workers had been laid off at that plant. At the same event, the president touted the fact that the deficit had been cut by two-thirds. What he didn't say was that under his watch the nation's debt had risen by $6 trillion. The true legacy of stimulus spending is not a stronger economy; it's much larger debt. As a country, we now owe more than $18 trillion, a figure that will burden taxpayers for decades to come.

If the stimulus program's main goal was to create work for Americans, it failed miserably. According to University of Maryland economist Peter Morici, by early 2015, one in six men of working age was unemployed. Obama had managed to create 7 million jobs (whereas 8.7 million had been lost in the recession), whereas President Ronald Reagan created 11 million jobs in a much smaller economy. In a rare meeting of the President's Jobs and Competitiveness Council, the president admitted that the plan to generate shovel-ready jobs wasn't a success. "Shovel-ready was not, uh, as shovel-ready as we expected," he said.

THE BANK OF WASHINGTON

The more of our federal tax dollars the president spent, the more it became clear that his goal wasn't just bailing out the economy but reordering it to fit his own version of the nation. Turning away from fossil fuels was a central part of that vision, no matter the cost.

The administration directed $14.5 billion in stimulus dollars to a loan guarantee program to finance the development of green energy technologies.

Solyndra, one of many solar panel makers funded by

the government, was the first to get a Department of Energy (DOE) loan, and the administration celebrated by sending the president for a photo op to the Fremont, California–based plant. Solyndra would showcase the administration's commitment to green energy and cutting-edge technology. We'd look supersmart! The event was a highly orchestrated production organized to spotlight the loan guarantee program. Presidential handlers decided that a robotic arm would be used to showcase the company's products. They told the company's chief executive not to wear a suit and asked another exec to wear a hard hat. The optics, the appearance of the event, was more important than the reality. And the reality was already dire. Days before the visit, investors were sending signals to DOE officials that Solyndra was tottering. By the end of that year, executives sought more help from what they called the Bank of Washington: taxpayer dollars.

Ultimately, Solyndra failed, squandering its $535 million loan. Adding insult to injury, taxpayers saw no return of those dollars when the company went into bankruptcy. Instead, a late investor in the company was given tax benefits of as much as $341 million, so-called tax loss carryforwards, by a bankruptcy judge. The insult was complete. Not only did taxpayers fail to reap a successful green energy company or jobs, but when Solyndra went bust, we recouped none of our investment. The Bank of Washington was a loser.

Failures such as Solyndra would be repeated over and over. Beacon Power, the second recipient in the loan guarantee program, declared bankruptcy after giving three executives more than a quarter of a million dollars in bonuses. BrightSource Energy squandered much of its $1.6 billion loan guarantee for a solar energy facility on a program to relocate desert tortoises.

Then there was Abound Solar, which received $400 million in federal loan guarantees. The Colorado company filed for bankruptcy just two years later, and its plant sat unoccupied, littered with hazardous waste, broken glass, and contaminated water. A local business group estimated that cleaning up the site would cost $3.7 million. One critic noted that if a coal, oil, or gas company had left behind the same mess, the Environmental Protection Agency (EPA) would have sent out SWAT teams to track down the offenders.

In winter 2011, the House held a series of hearings into the program's mismanagement. It became a show trial of the administration's management failures. Eighty percent of the federal program's dollars were directed to companies making solar panels, an industry dominated by the Chinese in which the players were discounting their products as a way to gain market share by the time the U.S. government decided to get involved. This was a mature business in which entrenched players could undercut new entrants. Any serious businessperson would have stayed away from putting taxpayers behind more solar panel energy production, but Uncle Sam, led by the Department of Energy, was eager to jump in.

In retrospect, the DOE's loan guarantee program looks

like just another failed government program. Clearly, the government miscalculated the demand for solar panels and misunderstood the industry's dynamics. Governments are notoriously bad at competing in the free market. But the mistakes went beyond poor business decision making. DOE bureaucrats bent the rules and ignored federal requirements that got in their way. In the end, the very people who had the biggest stake in making the federal government look like a prudent and efficient manager—its employees—were complicit in abusing the Bank of Washington.

DEPENDENCY CRISIS

It wasn't just pet projects such as the green energy program that got the go-ahead from the administration. The president's generosity with our taxpayer dollars expanded dramatically for welfare and poverty programs even after the recovery was in place. It became hard to square what was going on in the economy with the fact that we were technically in recovery mode. I remember my shock at the fact that the proportion of people receiving food stamps had swollen to one-sixth, or 47 million people, by September 2013—four years *into the recovery*. Unemployment peaked in 2010, but the food stamps rolls kept growing. For decades, the proportion of Americans receiving benefits had hovered between 8 percent and 11 percent because of restrictions on the length of time recipients could receive benefits, but things clearly had changed. I live in a pretty upscale neighborhood and had seen increasing numbers of people at my local grocery store paying the cashier with Supplemental Nutrition Assistance Program (SNAP) benefits. If this is Obama's economic expansion, I remembered thinking, I'd hate to see a recession.

Persistent high joblessness had propelled people into SNAP, but other factors had turned food stamps from a program that rose and fell with unemployment to a more permanent governmental feature of the landscape. Income and asset tests for applicants had been eased, allowing people with relatively high incomes and savings to get benefits, and the Obama administration encouraged states to loosen those standards. The idea? Give help to families before they fall into persistent poverty. To make that happen, the government encouraged people to apply even if they had savings or a low-wage job. In North Carolina, applicants earning 200 percent of the poverty level could receive monthly checks. The size of the benefits rose. And food stamps were just part of an emerging dependency crisis. The federal government spends $668 billion on 126 different antipoverty programs each year. State and local governments add $284 billion. In total, according to Michael Tanner at the Cato Institute, the United States spends nearly $1 trillion every year fighting poverty, or $20,610 per person on benefits or $61,830 per family of three.

No program grew faster during the recovery than Social Security Disability Insurance (SSDI), which was designed to help people with severe disabilities that keep them from working. Americans receiving the benefit rose to 11 million in September 2014 from 9 million in 2010. The tab for taxpayers was $260 billion annually. In fact, the Social Security Administration predicted in 2015 that the disability fund would go broke the next year because of that rapid-fire growth. A not insignificant cost of the program was legal fees to a growing number of lawyers who specialized in getting SSDI applications approved. The cost was $1.2 billion each year. More worrisome is the fact that once a person goes on SSDI, he or she is unlikely ever to rejoin the workforce. The Manhattan Institute estimates that fewer than 1 percent of program beneficiaries ever leave. If recipients were truly disabled that might be one thing, but according to former Senator Coburn, as many as 25 percent of recipients are not truly disabled and never should have been approved for benefits. The real risk of this abuse is that millions of truly disabled Americans could see their benefits cut while taxpayers get an increase in payroll taxes. The number of Americans on disability rose 19 percent faster than did jobs created during the recovery. How long this expansion of benefits can continue is a good question. Currently, there are just 1.65 employed persons in the private sector for every 1 person receiving welfare assistance, according to the American Enterprise Institute (AEI).

A deeper examination of antipoverty programs shows how ineffective they are. Fifty years after the War on Poverty was launched by Lyndon B. Johnson, the rate of poverty is almost exactly the same as it was in 1967. In other words, government programs have done very little to reduce the incidence of poverty in this country despite an expenditure of $22 trillion! Yes, $22 trillion, which is 22 with 12 zeros after it. To understand how much that is, according to the Heritage Foundation, if you laid a trillion one-dollar bills end to end, they would reach the sun and back 11 times. That's an incredible sum of money with very little to show for it.

My family is from a part of the country, western North Carolina, in which poverty was common. As a kid, I saw some of my relatives cope with no indoor plumbing; others lived in mobile homes. But that's not the face of poverty today. The actual living conditions of households labeled as poor by the U.S. Census Bureau are surprising to most people. According to the government's own surveys, 80 percent of poor households have air-conditioning, nearly two-thirds have cable or satellite television, half have a personal computer, and 40 percent have a wide-screen high-definition TV. Three-quarters own a car or truck, and nearly a third have two or more vehicles. When Johnson launched the programs, he advocated a "hand up, not a handout." Unfortunately, too often, these programs have morphed into the latter, and the taxpayer is the one who is penalized.

HEALTHCARE DEFORMATION

Wasting taxpayer dollars on existing programs is one thing, but the Obama administration also is creating entirely new programs that promise to hamstring our children with debt. Obamacare is exhibit number one. From a distance, it didn't look so bad. When it was passed back in March 2010, all you could see on the horizon at first were popular policy proscriptions such as "you can keep your children on your healthcare insurance policy until age 26 and insurers can't reject you for preexisting conditions." But as the ship sailed closer and closer, we began to see the real Obamacare up close, and it was clear it was an economic landmine for households and the federal government as well. My objections to the program are these: Not only does Obamacare raise the costs of government, it also raises healthcare costs for American families, offers them less choice, and goes a long way toward destroying the relationship of physician and family. This isn't healthcare reformation; it's healthcare deformation. Most people, however, didn't pay much attention to the Affordable Care Act until the rollout of the Obamacare web portal called Healthcare.gov on October 1, 2013.

It was a field day for critics. It's difficult to imagine Obamacare's implementation going any worse than it did. Although the president promised an experience as seamless as shopping on Amazon.com, attempting a transaction on the government's insurance website made a trip to the

Department of Motor Vehicles look like a field day. Truth is, Healthcare.gov rarely worked. Although 2.8 million people were said to have visited the website on its first day of operation, October 1, 2013, only 6 people succeeded in enrolling in healthcare plans. The site crashed repeatedly in those first weeks. Enrollees spent hours attempting to fill out online forms only to find that their information disappeared as the system crashed. Just accessing the site was difficult. Visitors often were met with a home page that told them the website was temporarily unavailable. Comparing plans' costs and offerings, which is essential to making an informed choice, was impossible. Were you eligible for a subsidy? You might have a difficult time finding out, and the numbers you received from the site could have been wrong. By November, the administration began taking the site down for entire weekends instead of just overnight for repairs. It became clear early on that Healthcare.gov had been launched before a thorough road test and met none of the performance standards consumers enjoyed on hundreds of private sector websites.

Yet after such a massive buildup to the launch of the president's signature legislation, failure was not an option, at least not an option officials would talk about publicly. When Health and Human Services Secretary Kathleen Sebelius attempted to defend the launch at a hearing called by a House panel that fall, she claimed Obamacare was working for "millions of Americans," a claim that strained credulity.

The website was down and inaccessible throughout her entire testimony. Cable channels broadcast a split screen of the hearing that day showing on one side the highly discomfited Sebelius muttering under her breath, "Don't do this to me," presumably to the Republicans grilling her, and on the other side the failed home page of the website. Likewise, when the president defended Healthcare.gov from the Rose Garden surrounded by a handful of people who had gotten coverage, he meekly offered that the site wasn't working as it should. But he didn't take responsibility. "Nobody's madder than me," he said, as if the problems were not his responsibility but someone else's. In the meantime, the president suggested that enrollees mail in their paperwork and hired another team to fix the site. Ultimately, the site alone would cost taxpayers $2.1 billion.

You'd expect that after a rocky start things would get better, but that didn't happen in this case. Implementation of the law continued to fail on many levels. Hundreds of thousands of Americans were told that their existing health insurance plans didn't meet Obamacare's strict requirements and that they would be forced to get new coverage. Grandfathering provisions were expected to protect millions of Americans for a short period, but the government reported that about half of all employer-sponsored plans (both large and small) would relinquish their protected status by the end of 2013. The reason? The healthcare law's one-size-fits-all approach required that all policies meet the same coverage requirements. As an example, a 60-year-old woman had to have access to maternity care. The requirement raises costs and reduces flexibility. As a result, the president's promise that "you can keep your plan" turned out to be just so much hot air. As confusion reigned, major insurers balked at participating in the exchanges that year, frustrated over the law's complexity and the erratic nature of its implementation. In the six months after the launch of Healthcare.gov, the administration announced it would delay or change enrollment and payment deadlines eight times.

Although Healthcare.gov served as the portal in 34 states, other states used state-built exchanges. Few state exchanges could claim to outpace Healthcare.gov. Maryland's website crashed on the day it opened, and the state ultimately decided there were too many bugs to fix and opted to move to a new system. Massachusetts, a state with experience in offering government-sponsored health insurance, launched a site riddled with errors and navigation problems. The governor was forced to offer a public apology. Minnesota's state plan, MNsure, had problems throughout its open enrollment period. Even California's program couldn't handle the high volume of calls, triggering long wait times.

No doubt the rollout of Healthcare.gov was troubled. But the real tragedy for Americans wasn't the glitches but the fact that Obamacare has raised healthcare costs for millions of people while promising to do just the opposite. The president in October 2013 had promised to give Americans "high

25

quality health insurance for less than the cost of your cell-phone bill," but that turned out to be simply not true. Obamacare coverage was no bargain. Monthly premiums averaged $328 a month by the second year of the law's implementation, which is four times more than the average monthly cell phone bill. And keep in mind that consumer costs don't stop with the premiums. As with any medical plan, coverage didn't kick in until enrollees had paid average annual deductibles of $2,550 to $5,000, which is at a minimum eight times a monthly cell phone bill and double the level of the average employer-sponsored deductible. Enrollees faced co-pays for drugs of as much as 40 percent. Worst hit were young enrollees, the so-called young invincibles the administration was desperate to claim. In fact, the entire success of the plan hinged on whether young people enrolled. But their costs were higher than those of private options by as much as 30 percent. Second-year cost estimates were even higher.

Bending the cost curve morphed into something else entirely during the economic malaise of 2013–2014. Rising prices discouraged healthcare use. People stopped going to the doctor as much or seeking care when it was optional because the cost was spiraling out of control. One in three said they or a family member had delayed medical care in 2014 because of those costs.

But if Obamacare failed to prove the bargain its authors anticipated, at least the healthcare law brought down costs in the private sector, right? The answer again is no. By

March 2013, health insurers privately warned the market that premiums for many individuals and small businesses would increase sharply because of the healthcare law, with some forecasting a doubling of rates. Policies backed by large companies also became increasingly expensive for workers, with average annual increases of 3 percent for premiums and deductibles as more companies began to plan ahead for the ultimate impacts of the Cadillac tax, a levy to reduce the government's backing of private health plans.

The financial impacts don't stop there. Most Americans who supported Obamacare had no idea of the increased taxes they'd be asked to pay to underwrite the president's landmark legislation. Among them are the individual mandate excise tax or fine, as the president likes to call it. Either way, if you don't have qualifying health insurance, you pay an income surtax of 2 percent in 2015 and 2.5 percent in 2016. This ultimately adds up to real money. There is also a 3.5 percent surtax on investment income for $200,000-plus earners ($250,000 for joint filers), plus higher dividend taxes. Then there are the adding-insult-to-injury tax code changes. Obamacare reduces the appeal of the highly popular health savings account and flexible savings account by eliminating the ability to use the savings on nonprescription medications. It also reduces the viability of the medical deduction for families facing high medical expenses from catastrophic diseases by upping the threshold for deductibility from 7.5 percent of adjusted gross income to 10 percent. And that's just to get started. There are a total of two dozen new or higher taxes, the worst of which is the Cadillac tax. This excise tax hits high-value healthcare plans and amounts to a 40 percent levy on individual plans with a value in excess of $10,200 and family plans valued at more than $27,500. Although the tax is levied on companies, it will be passed on to consumers as companies dial back their contributions to keep from hitting the tax thresholds. But because these thresholds are not adjusted for inflation, every year more and more plans will be defined as luxury Cadillac plans, and every year more people will face absorbing more of the costs on their own. Obama's goal is to stop subsidizing corporate healthcare plans that cover nearly half the population, a shocking policy change.

Already, the American Enterprise Institute estimates that Obamacare is the single biggest driver of entitlement spending by the government, which accounts for 49 percent of federal outlays. Spending on Obamacare will total $1.8 trillion over the next decade to cover its mandated expansion of Medicaid and subsidies for people purchasing insurance coverage on the exchanges. In other words, Obamacare didn't "bend the cost curve," the administration's phrase for cutting healthcare costs, but instead created entirely new government obligations that taxpayers will be forced to support in larger and larger amounts each and every year. Ironically, the president's own adviser, Jonathan Gruber, said that the law would ultimately be unaffordable even as he was helping the administration craft the legislation in 2009. He said that after he'd described Americans as being "too stupid" to figure out the changes. But those dramatic changes can't be hidden for long, and they will rebound negatively to American taxpayers and consumers of healthcare. In Chapter 4 I'll show you how Obamacare will compromise care for millions of Americans and what you can do to fight back and get the care and attention you deserve.

HOUSING

The failure of stimulus spending programs and Obama's signature healthcare legislation have received tons of media attention, but other programs enacted or approved by Obama have received little notice but hurt American wallets as well. The president doubled down on failed housing, education, and central bank policies that made life tougher for the middle class.

Housing policy matters because housing represents such a large proportion of the average family's net worth. According to the Federal Reserve, when the average couple retires, their biggest investment isn't a 401(k), pension, or IRA; it's their home. That's why the housing crash that erased $6.3 trillion in mortgage wealth from consumers' balance sheets was the toughest part of the Great Recession. Four million of us went into foreclosure. Housing prices fell by a third overall, more in some markets. The devastation was widespread, hitting poor neighborhoods and wealthy ones alike. Because of the price crash, millions of us ended up living in homes worth less than what we owed. Who is responsible for that pain? Well, I have news for you. It wasn't greedy banks bent on snatching our last dollar that authored that debacle. Sorry, Senator Elizabeth Warren. No, this disaster came thanks to government policy.

See, for decades the government via Fannie Mae, Freddie Mac, and the Federal Housing Administration pursued affordable housing goals that promoted loose bank underwriting standards. The idea was that expanding home ownership, especially among lower-income households, was an important national goal. Every president from Bill Clinton to George W. Bush to Barack Obama has participated eagerly. This level of involvement wouldn't have been possible without Fannie Mae and Freddie Mac, quasi-governmental entities that bought loans from banks and packaged them into investments. The two own or guarantee half of all mortgages in this country, some $5 trillion of consumer debt. Because of that deep involvement, the government could enforce its affordable housing goals. Banks were required to issue a certain proportion of loans with easy terms, low down payments, and loose debt-to-income requirements. Initially, government policy required that 30 percent of the mortgages purchased by Freddie and Fannie be made to low- and middle-income borrowers. During the Clinton administration that requirement was raised to 50 percent, and Bush raised the goal to 56 percent.

But these policies have backfired. Not only were the rules a major contributor to the housing crash—lax loans defaulted at a steep rate—they also failed in their goal of raising home ownership levels, which have fluctuated between 62 and 65 percent in recent years. Before these policies were enacted, home ownership rates were 63.9 percent. These affordable housing requirements are also responsible for raising prices and reducing the very affordability they sought to increase. Here's how that works: The lower the down payment requirement is, the bigger and more expensive houses buyers can afford. At 10 percent, a buyer with $10,000 can afford a $100,000 home. But drop the down payment requirement to 5 percent and the same buyer can upgrade to a $200,000 home. Therefore, prices rise and affordability wanes.

Obama has added fuel to the fire. Tighter regulations enacted because of the housing crash were abandoned at the administration's direction. Regulators had required a down payment of 20 percent and maximum debt-to-income ratios of 36 percent. Instead, under Obama's watch, down payment requirements returned to 3 percent and debt-to-income limits rose to 43 percent. Mel Watt, a North Carolina legislator whom Obama appointed to run the government's housing policy, is a longtime affordable housing advocate who continues to push the very affordable housing goals that got us in trouble in the first place. In Chapter 7 we'll look at how you can profit from real estate and sidestep the disasters promoted by a progressive housing policy.

EDUCATION

Fewer price tags sting middle-class families more these days than the price of college. Tuition and fees are on a rocket ride higher. Even during the recession, our nation's colleges and universities kept right on instituting price hikes. Annual tuition inflation continues to perk along at 3 to 4 percent above the broader economy's inflation. CourseSmart estimates that over the last 30 years tuition costs have risen 1,120 percent, whereas healthcare has gone up just 600 percent and housing has risen 375 percent. An education is four times as expensive as it was 30 years ago. These days, a single year at a public institution can run you $22,261 if you count everything from room and board to beer. If you don't qualify for scholarships, it's easy for a four-year tab to run into six figures. If gas prices rose this quickly, there'd be a move in Congress to tap the Strategic Petroleum Reserve. Remember when students would take jobs and pay for school as they learned? You can't do that now.

It's no surprise, then, that total student debt tops $1 trillion and that the average grad enters the workforce (if he or she is lucky) with $33,000 in debt. College debt is taking a toll on Mom and Dad too. People over 60 hold $36 billion in college debt. College debt is dogging generations of Americans, with no end in sight.

There are all kinds of reasons for this inflation. Yes, college bureaucracies are burgeoning and pay is rising. Annual salary hikes of presidents of public universities tick along at 5 percent, and the median pay package was $441,392 in 2012, plus the ranks of college bureaucrats deepen every year. Also, more schools compete with one another for students by boosting amenities. Finer gyms, sushi bars, and climbing walls suck up an ever increasing amount of higher ed dollars. Richard Vedder, who directs the Center for College Affordability and Productivity and teaches economics at Ohio University, describes the situation as an "economic arms race."

Even so, none of this would be possible without the billions of loans floated by the federal government to bankroll education. Basically, the federal student loan agency, Sallie Mae, bankrolls any degree anytime. If you can fog a mirror in this country, you can get a college loan backed by federal taxpayers. This lack of restraint means that unlike virtually every other consumer product there is no ceiling for college tuition and fees.

In a world in which a product—yes, even education is a product—is unmoored from economic limits, runaway inflation is inevitable. But the Obama policies have made the situation worse, not better. First, the president decided to make loan forgiveness more accessible. As a result, not only were there no limits on borrowing, it has become easier and easier to escape from college debt. Obama's Pay as You Earn program lowers monthly payments to make loans more affordable for graduates. Specifically, college grads who meet income eligibility standards need to pay only 10 percent of their discretionary income for 20 years. What's more, if grads work for the government or in "public service," they pay for 10 years and after that the loan is forgiven. Imagine the grad who stays in school to avoid a punk job market and winds up piling up $100,000 in loans. He or she goes to work for a nonprofit (public service) and earns very little and pays very little. Under the president's plan, the loan would be forgiven after 10 years at a point when the former student owes more than the original $100,000 balance because the payments were so low that the loan had negative amortization. This is no way to run an education system and sends the wrong message to students—that you can always game the system to get what you want without paying for it.

But wait, things get worse. In January 2015, the president proposed giving high school grads a free ride for two years at a community college. A free ride for two years! Forget whether community colleges have the capacity to handle such a program; taxpayer costs would be astonishing. With about 8 million students attending community college and paying $3,800 a year in tuition and fees, one can estimate that the president's generosity with our money would cost at minimum $30.4 billion. No doubt, eliminating the price tag also would devalue the education. After all, who wants to hire the student who got the Uncle Sam degree? Is it as good as a private education? And wouldn't such a program ultimately raise the baseline of costs for all higher education? After all, if Uncle Sam is footing the bill, what's the incentive for community college administrators to hold the line on tuition?

The free community college proposal reveals the problem at the heart of so many Obama policies: money solves every problem, and there is an endless stream of taxpayer dollars available. Ultimately, limitless loans mean colleges and universities face no pressure against pushing rising costs onto students. The costs of education will continue to rise, and the middle class will be expected to shoulder the burden. In Chapter 3 we'll examine strategies for locking down a college education at an affordable cost.

THE FED

Few of us spend much time thinking about the mysterious Federal Reserve, but the central bank plays an enormous role in the financial lives of everyday Americans because it sets interest rates, the price of money. President Obama is charged with appointing both the members of the Board of Governors and the chair of the Fed.

The bank's mandate is large. Its job is to keep the

monetary and financial system stable. In recent years, it exercised enormous power to do just that. In the wake of the 2006 financial crisis, the Fed printed money, created dollars electronically out of thin air, and gave that money to failing banks directly as loans. The Fed also bought trillions of dollars' worth of banks' failed investments in the housing market in a program called quantitative easing that began in November 2008 and continued until fall 2014. Buying those bonds put money into the economy and created a market demand for those products where none existed.

But no policy had a more immediate and negative impact on American's wallets than its decision to keep interest rates at virtually zero for seven years. The policy was initiated by Ben Bernanke and continued by Obama's appointee to the helm of the Federal Reserve, Janet Yellen. This kind of stimulus has never been tried in American history. The closest example is the period 1942–1951, when the Fed was ordered to make it easy for the government to borrow at low rates to pay off war debt. You could call this policy a tax on savers because it robbed the middle class of any return on savings. Interest rates on the basic tools of savings for middle-class families—certificates of deposit and savings accounts—couldn't overcome the low rates of inflation during the recovery. Money actually lost value for savers under these conditions. Holders of money market funds suffered in exactly the same way. Millions of people who diligently saved and opted to take care of themselves now have little to show for a lifetime of effort. Make no mistake, this is a tragedy. People 75 and older get 8 percent of their income from interest on investments. The rest is largely government programs such as Social Security. For them, America has truly become the land of no returns. According to *Forbes*, the $12 trillion in short-term savings investments has lost 10 percent over the period during which the Fed has been stabilizing the system. This was essentially another wealth transfer from the federal government. But now the people on the short end of the stick are the people who can least afford it: those close to and already in retirement.

The trouble caused by low rates extends beyond conventional savings vehicles to other products. Retirees looking to lock in guaranteed returns by buying fixed annuities saw their nest eggs dwindle. That occurred because monthly income falls with interest rates that exist at the time of purchase. Similarly, the responsible folks who want to pay their own nursing home bills and opt to buy long-term-care insurance have faced spiking premiums. That is the case because insurers have to raise prices when interest rates fall. Pension plans also suffer from low rates. With 80 percent of corporate pensions already underfunded, anemic returns at the short end of the yield curve make it more difficult for risk-averse pension managers to make money for retirees.

Low rates have been a double-edged sword for Americans. For borrowers, they've been a blessing, but if you were attempting to find a safe haven for your nest egg, you would have lost out. In Chapter 6 we'll look at ways savers can improve returns and still not take on too much risk.

CONCLUSION

As a college student at Miami University in Ohio, I had the sense that the possibilities were many. I knew I was limited only by my abilities. Truth is, I graduated into a deep recession, but I still felt I had the opportunity to succeed if I applied myself.

I feel those opportunities still exist for Americans. Although it's been tough to watch the transformation of this country from one that was dynamic and expanding to one that increasingly looks to government to solve its problems, the best prepared among us will still succeed and do well. Throughout this book, I'll show you strategies to help overcome the malaise and lack of confidence that plague so many of us. You'll discover fresh strategies for achieving the American dream and learn ways to secure a solid future for your family.

2

WHY THE PATH TO
WEALTH IS NOT CLOSED

It's quite possible that after reading Chapter 1 you have come to the conclusion that it is simply impossible for you to be a financial success on your own. Maybe you sense that the headwinds are too strong. America has changed and not for the good, you think. Opportunity is a thing of the past in this country. The great American dream might have been attainable for a previous generation, but not today. I disagree. I believe success is still possible for those who are persistent, pay attention to the details, and take advantage of the opportunities that come their way or make their own. Truth is, today's economy requires a different mind-set to be successful. You'll have to beat the Washington bureaucrats at their own game, to be sure, but you'll also have to curb your worst impulses and take the long view. You'll need to be more focused and open to new solutions to old problems.

I'm going to start by rebuilding your confidence in the system so that you can see your way forward to becoming a financial success. I think this is an essential first step for many of us. Then we'll take a clear-eyed view of where you stand right now. If you want to build wealth and become a financial success, you'll need to analyze your current situation and make sure you are ready for the biggest financial challenges you are likely to face. I'll help you start the journey toward getting your finances in hand and on track.

First things first. Let's take on the confidence issue. Central to the American way of life, I believe, is the idea that you own your successes. As a nation, we believe that individuals author their own accomplishments, and it's this idea that fuels so much economic energy and so many powerful new ideas. You own it, and you benefit from your own labor. That's why when the president commented, "If you've got a business, you didn't build that. Somebody else made that happen," so many of us were deeply offended. His viewpoint is strange to the ears of most Americans.

The truth is that Americans of many stripes are creating their own successes every day and benefiting from them. The benefits of innovations in social media and mobile apps are flowing to coders who sidestepped college to make their fortunes early. The fracking revolution, which has done what no Congress could do by boosting our energy independence and upending energy markets, was led largely by small entrepreneurs who often took advantage of mineral rights their families had held for decades. ExxonMobil didn't lead this renaissance, and neither did K Street, and the benefits are pouring directly into the pockets of families all over the country. Every day, Americans are making it on their own and putting together their own financial future through the fruits of their own labor as plumbers, car salespersons, alpaca farmers, and every manner of vocation.

It's simply not true that *only* the top 1 percent of Americans are getting ahead these days. The centerpiece of the Left's economic agenda has been that the gains of the top 1 percent have come at the expense of the vast majority of Americans, and we have pretty much swallowed this idea whole. The idea is so pervasive that many of us, when polled, assert we are lower middle class. But the numbers show that this country is still producing wealthy individuals in large numbers. And by that I don't mean billionaires. I mean solid high-net-worth upper-middle-class families that continue to find success and establish a future for themselves. In a single year, 2014, our economy minted 496,945 new millionaires, a 9.5 percent gain over 2014 and a better rate of growth of high-net-worth families than China, Brazil, the United Kingdom, or Russia, according to data from WealthInsight. This explosion in millionaires brought the total number of wealthy individuals in this country to 5.2 million. That's five times the number of millionaires in China, which has four times the population of the United States. The United States can claim 32 times the number of millionaires in Russia. Even during the president's first term of office, 1.1 million Americans joined the $1 million club, and by 2017 the nation will boast nearly 17 million households with a net worth of $1 million. Fidelity Investments, the huge retirement account administrator, tracked 1,100 individuals whose 401(k) plans were worth $1 million or more over a dozen years. The average salary for the members of this group, who were at the peak of their earning years at an average age of 59, was no more than $150,000 a year, a tidy sum but certainly not enough to earn membership in the 1 percent club.

By now I hope you're feeling a little more upbeat about your potential and considering taking the reins of your future. You *can* be a financial success. Other people are succeeding, and you can as well. One of the tricks of getting there is managing your finances well over time. The folks in the Fidelity survey had some fascinating habits in common. First off, they started saving early, often in their twenties. Accumulating savings early gives investors that much more time to grow their money. Remember, the first $100,000 is the hardest to save and takes the longest to accumulate. At that level, gains can be seen and holders start getting the sense that they are making progress. The earlier you can hit this tipping point, the better. Because of an early start, these people were able to drive their balances to $400,000 by their late forties. This group also wasn't shy about investing in stocks, putting 70 percent of their portfolios in equities. Another key to success is that the members of this group saved a median of 14 percent of their pay annually, or $13,300 a year, not including company matches. With the employer match, the investors' total set-aside was 19 percent of pay! It's hard not to be successful at that level. Thus first you have to have the foresight and the determination to get started, and then you have to manage your money well over time.

Now THAT you understand the lay of the land, let's evaluate where you are. Let's take off the rose-colored glasses most of us wear and take a look at the most important measures of financial success. Are you on track to retire? By that I don't just mean that you are making regular contributions to a retirement account. The story for most of us is that we are severely underprepared. Financial journalists cheered when Fidelity announced that the average 401(k) balances among its clients hit $91,300 at the end of 2014, a 30 percent jump from 2011. But that level wouldn't sustain an average household for three years in retirement. In short, you're going to need more.

I understand that you'll be contributing different amounts depending on your age. When it comes to retirement savings, the typical trajectory for 401(k) contributions is small at the beginning and larger at the end as you earn more money. Early in your career, the absolute dollars you set aside may seem small, but this is the critical foundation on which your savings will be built. Fidelity offers a useful rule of thumb. By age 36, for example, you should have saved one times your current salary; by age 45, three times your salary; and by age 55 five times your salary. Are your savings even close to that? These numbers may seem impossibly high, but consider that you're more likely to experience periods of unemployment in today's job market. The Great Recession taught us that layoffs are a reality of today's job market. Plus, you'll be saving for what may be a retirement that is decades longer than your parents' as longevity rises. And don't forget that healthcare costs are on a constant march higher. For more details on saving successfully for retirement, check out Chapter 6.

The biggest obstacle to hitting your goals is not setting aside enough to begin with. You must resist the temptation to cash out your retirement in the early years. More than half of workers in their twenties who have 401(k) plans do just that. They cash out their holdings when they change jobs, partly because their balances are relatively low, according to benefits consultant Aon Hewitt. Only about a third of those who change jobs in their fifties do this. Taking the money and running, even when you have only a little set aside, is a mistake because you'll have to start your savings all over again and will miss out on the gains you would have made had you stayed in the market. My advice is that even in your twenties you should pretend that your retirement money has been spent and is not accessible. Remember, if you've tapped your retirement dollars at any point in your savings history, you are behind. Even if you paid that money back, which you are required to do if you borrow from your 401(k), you had less time to allow that money to grow.

That's the problem for many of us. We are playing catch-up. We haven't been funding a 401(k) for our entire working lives, we've borrowed from it, or we've put in a paltry sum. For that reason, I believe many of us may have to set aside savings in a 401(k) plus open a second account, such as a Roth IRA, to make sure we have the funds we need at retirement. Set aside 12 to 15 percent of your income at a minimum if you want to be financially independent.

The next item on our checklist is backup. You need to make sure that if something bad happens, you are prepared. Do you have a six-month emergency savings account? That's a full half year in earnings that you need to set aside in a fund you can access quickly. This saves you from bankruptcy if you unexpectedly lose your job or face medical problems. A garden-variety home repair has the potential to send the average household into financial disarray if that family doesn't have savings. I remember well how handy our savings account was when a massive red oak fell in our yard. Our insurer would not pay for disposing of the tree, which turned out to be a $14,000 job. Sure, we could have tapped our retirement fund or taken out a home equity line of credit, but we had savings, and that allowed us to take care of the problem with no interest costs or penalties. Having an emergency fund is also a great way to assert financial control. If you know that you have insurance, you'll be less likely to stay in a job that is a poor fit. Money means command over your life, and that is a confidence builder.

The other big financial goal for most families is paying for their children's college education. Parents often wonder whether they have enough savings set aside for their children's education, and it's no wonder why. Costs for education have escalated faster than inflation for decades. (See Chapter 3 for more detailed information on college education.) In this chapter I will help you evaluate your savings to see if you are on track. Consider this: If you are saving $32.57 a week, or $130.28 a month, it will take 17 years to save $50,000 if you earn 6 percent on your money. It will take savings of $54.76 a week, or $219.04 a month, if you have just 12 years to earn $50,000 at the same rate of return. It will take $93.71 a week, or $374.84 a month, to save $50,000 at a 6 percent rate of interest if you wait until you have just eight years to save. And if you have only four years to save $50,000, you'll need to set aside $212.83 a week, or $851.32 a month. Let's face it, it's not likely that $50,000 is going to cover the entire college education tab. Remember, it's not the cost of today's education that matters here (exorbitant though it may be) but the price tag your children will encounter when they start their first day as a freshman, after 5, 10, or 15 years of college inflation. The point is that the longer you wait, the more you will need. If you are smart enough to start when your child is born, $300 a month will get you close to paying for a state-school education. (You'll need more if you send them to a private school or an out-of-state public university.)

One critical warning for parents: as you consider your college savings balances, be careful not to give all your money to your kids. Financial advisers tell me they are astonished at how much money moms and dads are giving their grown children. After all, your kids can borrow for their education. You can't borrow your retirement dollars.

If you remember anything from this chapter, it should be this: becoming financially successful is a goal worth achieving, and it can still happen in this great country. It can happen to you if you work and strive toward it with a goal firmly in mind. But it takes planning and hard work. What you find, though, as you watch people who are successfully moving toward this goal is that they have a handful of positive characteristics in common. They know the value of money and are loath to waste it. They make their own luck, and they aren't flummoxed by failure; in fact, they see it as inevitable and a good teacher. They don't compare themselves with the neighbors but set their own standards.

What's more, the United States is the best place on this planet to get ahead on one's own. We have faced adversity multiple times and come back. After all, only 15 years ago we experienced the worst attack on our shores since Pearl Harbor when Osama bin Laden attacked the World Trade Center Towers and the Pentagon, killing 3,000 Americans on September 11, 2001. President George W. Bush went to the World Trade Center site, clambered on the rubble, and swore our enemies would hear from us. And they did. Weeks later, we were fighting bin Laden in the frozen mountains of Afghanistan. And though the attack occurred in New York City, the center of our nation's economic activity, Wall Street did not fall. It repaired itself, and now trading occurs on electronic platforms all over the country. No one attack could stop our markets today. The point is that America has a core of toughness and resilience to call upon. And so, by extension, do you.

3

GETTING AN
AFFORDABLE EDUCATION

It never ceases to amaze me what my friends spend to raise their children. Between the child care, private schools, food, and clothing, it's no wonder that in so many families both parents work. The Department of Agriculture estimates the average cost of raising a child born in 2012 to age 18 at $241,080, or $301,970 if you factor in inflation. Shockingly, that doesn't include the cost of a college education. Parents in big coastal cities spend far, far more. In the New York area, some parents spend $19,000 a year on nursery school! Yes, parents have it hard. And then, just as they should be doubling down on retirement savings, they face the hefty and growing tab for college. Average tuition costs at the nation's universities are rising at a steadier clip than any other consumer good in the economy. Public (in-state) annual college tuition averaged $8,655 in 2014, and in out-of-state public colleges it averaged $21,706 *each year.* Attendees at private four-year colleges paid even more: $29,056 on average. But tuition is just the beginning of your nightmare. Housing, food, textbooks, beer, and pizza can double tuition costs. Your total four-year tab can easily stretch into six figures. The average total costs at the most expensive private colleges and universities can run close to $65,000 a year. When I was in college, my work-study earnings helped my family close the affordability gap, but that's hardly possible now.

Parents are in a panic. My friend Allison says that when her oldest daughter entered high school, she started waking every night with the same nightmare. In it, her daughter attended a local college for four years, but when it was time to graduate, she was denied her diploma because Allison couldn't make the last tuition payment. She's not alone in panicking over college costs.

If you're worried you can't afford the education you feel your child or grandchild deserves, read on. In this chapter I'll get to the bottom of how liberal progressive policies have pushed the price tag out of reach and what you can do to finesse college aid officers and the system to get a quality education for your family. You'll learn how to navigate the bloated academic-industrial complex (as I call the higher education system) and pay for college without going broke.

Strangely, a college education is the only thing I know of that our society has agreed should have no cost constraints. People balk at paying $4 for a gallon of milk, but a $150,000 tab for an Ivy League education is just fine. Average annual tuition inflation perks along at 3 to 4 percent above the broader economy's inflation, and that means that even if you start college planning when Tommy is a toddler, your actual costs may be far different from what you anticipate. Over the last 30 years, tuition costs have risen 1,120 percent while healthcare has gone up just 600 percent and housing has risen 375 percent. The Pell Grant, a $5,500 per semester federal award for low-income families originally designed to pick up most of the tab for school, today barely makes a dent in college costs. An education is 12 times more expensive than it was 30 years ago. Things have gotten so out of hand that several states offer aid to middle- and upper-middle-class families. California offers to foot 40 percent of the education tab for families earning up to $150,000 a year, and in Minnesota families earning $120,000 can get $5,000 in aid.

The toll on American families is heavy. Total student loan debt for the country is $1.2 trillion, and the average grad entering the workforce after graduation in 2014 carried a debt load of $33,000, an all-time high. Paying back that debt is forcing grads to delay marrying, having children, and buying a first home. Fifty-one percent of student loans are in deferment or forbearance, which means that the borrowers have agreed to pay the debt later, after even more interest costs have accrued. In other words, students are digging themselves into a deeper and deeper debt hole. These days, though, it isn't just the grads who are at risk. Mom, Dad, and even grandparents find their pockets tapped. People over 60 hold $36 billion in college debt, and it's this age category in which debt is growing the fastest.

Economists say that prices in any marketplace naturally reset lower when buyers evaporate because of high costs, but that hasn't happened in higher education. Why not? By far, the biggest reason college costs have skyrocketed is the easy money available to students and parents in the form of government-guaranteed student loans. For that reason, higher prices haven't taken customers out of the system. If you can fog a mirror, you can get up to $12,500 every year in student loans. The government requires no credit checks on applicants. None. This makes for a rising tide of tuition dollars for schools. Not surprisingly, college administrators opt to raise prices. And for that reason, more and more students find it easier and easier to take out loans not just to cover tuition and books but also to pay for rent, beer, and pizza under the federal category heading "living expenses." Consider the case of the 30-year-old Florida sales clerk who enrolled in a community college so that he could get student loans, using them to pay rent to a relative, finance his entertainment, and pay his cell phone bills while he attended community college part-time. This was his second go-round. He'd already gotten a degree in public relations using student loans but hadn't been able to find a job in that field. Now, by staying in school he could delay repaying his first loan while accruing more debt. At last check, he was studying to be an actor. This would be funny if it weren't so tragic. He says he needs to stay in school to make ends meet, but clearly he is delaying the inevitable next step of paying off his escalating debt.

Think abusing the system is uncommon? Think again. As the economic recovery failed to provide job opportunities for grads, more and more of them opted to spend more time in school and borrow more money. Online students, according to a report from the Department of Education's inspector general, are the worst culprits. According to the report, some 42,000 students received an average of $5,285 from online schools in loan money even though they weren't logging any credits at the time. A lot of this overborrowing is the result of fraud, but according to Edvisors, in 2011 about a quarter of students took out loans that exceeded their tuition by $2,500. Sixty-eight percent of all undergraduate borrowers hit the annual loan ceiling, up from 60 percent in 2008.

The solutions put forward by Obama's administration only double down on debt as the solution to rising college costs. The most pernicious is the student loan forgiveness program called Pay as You Earn. The program expands debt forgiveness for students who meet income eligibility standards. The rules go like this: You pay 10 percent of your discretionary income for a maximum of 20 years. Discretionary income is defined as the amount you earn above the poverty line for your family size. If the borrower's job is in public service, government work, or nonprofit work, he or she pays only for 10 years. After that, the debt simply disappears. Poof! Or that's what the liberals would like you to believe. Truth be told, it *doesn't* disappear. The debt becomes part of the federal debt to be paid for by taxpayers. This fact came sharply into focus in February 2015 when readers of the president's budget realized that his new forgiveness program already had resulted in a $21.8 billion deficit in the student loan program, a debt bigger than the annual budget for NASA or the EPA. Over the next decade, the program is expected to add another $250 billion to the nation's deficit. Sadly, there is still no free lunch.

The same goes for the president's idea of giving every American child two free years of community college. That $20 billion proposal, which was shot down almost as soon as it was proposed, would guarantee two free years of education for students, essentially expanding government-funded education from kindergarten through a two-year degree. Although the president said he envisioned a program accessible to any student willing to "work for it," the standard for participation was set low at a 2.5 grade point average. Even education experts scoffed at this idea, saying that community colleges don't have the capacity to handle an onslaught of new students. Further, according to Robert Archibald, Chancellor Professor of Economics at the College of William & Mary, such a program ultimately could empty classrooms on university campuses that rely on tuition dollars from undergrads who fill larger first-year and second-year classrooms to keep costs down. Wouldn't that lead to even higher tuition on conventional campuses? As with so many Obama programs, the negative unintended consequences are punishing.

Now, you might be thinking that loan forgiveness or free community college ultimately would be a positive for students by reducing their debt burdens. If *Rich Is Not a Four-Letter Word* is on the side of students, shouldn't we support it? The fact is, I'm on the side of the *whole* family. Ultimately, Obama's programs would raise the costs of government for taxpayers while making Uncle Sam more intrusive in our daily lives. Who is to say that a government funding education might not decide to limit what you could study? Remember, the current administration plowed taxpayer dollars into solar panels at a time when opportunities were slim. I think it's highly likely government would back curriculum choices that would similarly favor trendy, of-the-moment technologies that might or might not bear fruit in the long run. What's more, some parents may not want to choose two years of community college. Why should their desires be ignored? Choice is an important part of education. The president's one-size-fits-all solution just doesn't satisfy on any level.

None of his education proposals, though, were more confounding than his idea to eliminate the tax benefits of 529 college savings plans. Expanded under President George W. Bush, the savings accounts allowed parents to set aside money for education and withdraw that money without paying taxes when it was used for education expenses. This program promotes college savings by families instead of encouraging them to find a government-based solution. The savings aren't guaranteed by the federal government as loans are, but the government keeps its hands off the proceeds to encourage Americans to save. When Obama proposed taxing these accounts as part of his 2014 State of the Union plan to assist the middle class, he described 529s as a perk of the elite. But the facts argue otherwise. If the accounts had been the preserve of the elite, you would have expected their total numbers to be small and the average account balances to be high. Yet when the president attacked 529s, 7 *million* families maintained accounts, with an average balance of $19,774. Seventy percent of 529 plans were owned by households with incomes below $150,000. Average monthly contributions were $175, hardly the way Richie Rich's trust fund ran. The outcry against Obama's attack on college savings was sure and swift, and the administration quickly pulled back the proposal. Thank goodness!

Despite all the nonsensical ideas coming out of Washington, real solutions are being employed successfully all over the country to combat the high cost of education. When Mitch Daniels, the former governor of Indiana, took over as president of Purdue University, he froze tuition, a rare move and one especially foreign to the West Lafayette, Indiana, campus, where tuition had risen in each of the previous 36 years. When I interviewed Daniels, he told me he took a red pencil and eliminated spending on "low hanging fruit, commonsense things." "Purdue is no different from a lot of other universities," he said. "They raised prices because they could." He changed the campus health plan to a less expensive option and managed the university's cash more efficiently. Everything was evaluated. A fleet of 10 school cars was sold (about $10,000 each), rental storage was cut in half ($160,000 saved), and office furniture was reused instead of replaced ($28,000 saved).

As a result of his paying closer attention to costs that didn't affect education, the overall cost of attendance at Purdue went down for the first time on record. The cost of meal plans was cut 10 percent, and room rates flattened. A partnership with Amazon allowed Purdue students to save $25 million on textbooks over four years. Student borrowing declined 18 percent after borrowers were counseled about the dangers of debt. Even more impressive is the fact that it took Daniels just 19 months to make those changes.

The experience at Purdue should give you hope that the winds of change are blowing. But most parents and students still struggle with the academic-industrial complex. Unlike almost any private sector business, the nation's colleges and universities are bloated with costs, many of which have little to do with providing quality education. Even Purdue has 75 percent more administrators and staff on the payroll than it did 13 years ago, and it's not alone. According to Richard Arum, the coauthor of *Academically Adrift*, a serious critique of the education establishment, the fastest-growing category of professional employment in higher education is nonfaculty support professionals, in other words, bureaucrats. Compensation for the paper pushers is growing. On average, college and university presidents' compensation is about $500,000, with many making $1 million a year. That kind of pay inflation leads to $800,000 pay packages for provosts and $500,000 deans.

Surely, you may think, all this spending means the level of instruction has gotten better? Not so much. Students have less and less access to the brains of the game: professors. Only 40 percent of students are being taught by tenure-track instructors. Despite a wave of federal funding, recent government reports show that the proportion of full-time instructional faculty declined from 78 percent in 1970 to 52 percent in 2005. Professors spend less time teaching and preparing to teach or advising students and more time writing and researching. Arum says the average time dedicated to students is just 11 hours per week. Students' performance reflects their effort. Today's full-time college students spend just 13 hours a week studying compared with 25 hours in 1961 and 20 hours in 1981.

More and more of the billions of dollars in rising tuition fees is spent on things that won't advance the education experience. Instead, the money is frittered away on elaborate student unions, workout facilities with "lazy rivers," and showcase campuses. "It's an academic arms race," says

Richard Vedder, who directs the Center for College Afford-ability and Productivity and teaches economics at Ohio University. Schools increasingly compete for the best stu-dents by installing the most attractive infrastructure. Says Vedder, "Even classroom buildings have to have atriums; if not, it's downscale." There are schools that do laundry for their students or offer valet service for students who need to get to class ASAP. Is it any wonder that students are highly satisfied with their experience on campus? Surveys show a satisfaction rate of 90 percent. Who in her right mind would ever want to graduate?

Maybe this would be acceptable if students were emerg-ing from school better prepared for the workforce and more grown up, able to reason, write, and, in short, lead. The facts, though, tell a different story. Arum reports that *a third of students* gain no measurable skills during four years of college. None. He came to these conclusions after surveying 2,000 students in the largest study of its kind, tracking those students through college and into the labor force and mea-suring their abilities for critical thinking, complex reasoning, and writing. It's no surprise, then, that despite laying out tens of thousands of dollars in tuition and living expenses, many students can't get or keep jobs. More than 115,000 janitors have bachelor degrees, says Vedder, who estimates that a million retail clerks are in the same boat along with 15 percent of taxi drivers. "We're turning out too many anthro-pologists and not enough truck drivers," he says.

NO MORE THAN FOUR YEARS

Why am I cataloging the many failures of today's higher education system? Because if you've been busy raising children for 18 years, you may be unaware of how much college campus life—its costs and payoffs—has changed. You need to know what you are up against. Too many parents are simply ignorant of the problems. When I talk to mothers about the process of choosing a school for their son or daughter, I often get a misty-eyed response. Parents are more prone than their potential college students to romanticize the process, imagining a *Love Story* world in which their offspring will engage in Socratic debate by day and hole up in the library stacks at night. That's not what's going on today on campus. Mom and Dad need to get with the program and realize the financial cliff they may be walking off if their child performs even close to norms. If there is only one number you remember from this chapter, it should be this: *just 39 percent of college students graduate in four years.* After five years, 55 percent of the average class has gotten a sheepskin, and after six years, it's only 60 percent. Each year you wait for Joanie to graduate, it's another $23,000 or so out the window. Job number one for Mom and Dad is to make sure that their matriculating college student knows that the slow train to a degree is not one they are going to take. If you want your child or grandchild to be surrounded by students eager to complete a degree, check out the *Chronicle of Higher*

Education's website and its college completion calculator. There you'll learn whether the schools you're targeting have a good track record of graduating students in four years.

To ensure that your child graduates in four years, your prospective student should have some idea of what he or she wants to study. Sampling multiple fields is a waste of time. Prospective students should be narrowing their choices in high school with part-time work and internships. As a high school student, I learned a lot about media by writing a column for my local newspaper. The worst scenario is when the parent picks a course of study for a student. One family I know tried to force a young man into prelaw. His father believed a law degree was the route to success and riches. Unfortunately, his son was not interested in pursuing a law degree or any degree at all. After flunking out of two schools, he trained as a paramedic and firefighter and ended up pursuing a highly successful career serving his community. He's the most popular guy in town and happy to boot. Unfortunately, Mom and Dad had to pay the price for that lesson. Bottom line: watch out for the square peg, round hole problem. It can be expensive.

Getting value for your dollars when it comes to education means taking off the rose-colored glasses and realizing that even though many of these colleges and universities are covered in ivy, they are businesses determined to separate tuition dollars from your wallet. No college administrator is going to stop little Johnny from stretching out his undergrad experience another year or two, and Purdue's program of advising students to take on less debt is not the norm. Think of the student aid officers you talk to as the college's first line of defense. Their job is to give you the least amount of money they can in grants and scholarships and still get your child in the front door. Because student enrollments are down and acceptance rates (except at the elite colleges) are up, the real hurdle today for parents isn't getting their children accepted to college but paying the enormous tab.

WHY YOU SHOULD IGNORE THE STICKER PRICE

Finally, some good news. Even if your son or daughter has his or her heart set on an expensive Ivy League school, such as Princeton, or Stanford, the price published in university guides may not be the price most students at that hallowed institution are paying. The average grant to freshmen at Princeton is $35,700. That's free money! At MIT the freshman grant averages $36,200, and at Stanford it's $40,500. Similar gaps between published prices and reality exist at many of the nation's colleges and universities. In fact, Rob Franek, an author and the *Princeton Review*'s senior vice president, says that only a third of students pay full tuition costs. Don't regard the eye-popping tally of frosh costs your son or daughter handed you as the last word. In fact, it's more like the sticker price, the suggested payment that college administrators hope you fall for. Paying for college these days isn't a matter of making good on their wish list but putting one together that works for you. The bottom line here is that you should not drop all the expensive colleges from consideration, because you may get a great financial package from one of them. How much debt should your son or daughter be willing to take on? Most experts say that newly minted grads shouldn't enter the workforce with more than the amount of their starting annual salary in student loan debt. I know this sounds impossible, but here's how that calculation works: It will take your son or daughter 10 years to pay off debt equivalent to his or her starting annual salary. If the debt is twice that salary level, it will take 20 years to pay it down.

The reality for many college administrators is that they are competing mightily for a declining number of students. Enrollments in 2012 fell by half a million students for the first time since 2006, according to the Census Bureau. That means you have leverage when it comes to your total tab. In today's environment, don't assume a large state or public school is the best option. Even with a higher sticker price, a small private school may give your son or daughter more free money. In fact, according to the National Association of College and University Business Officers, 70 percent of all grant aid to undergraduate students attending a private nonprofit college was provided by the schools. However, be aware that some schools are facing financial shortfalls. More than one expert in higher education finance has told me that a small number of the nation's 4,495 degree-granting institutions may not be around in four years because of declining state funding and enrollment. The last thing you want to do is pick an institution because of its great aid package only to find out it's not open the next year. And watch out for a new tactic used by out-of-state public schools. With federal aid dollars dwindling, they are looking to make up the difference by admitting more out-of-state students who pay higher tuition bills. That "safety school" plan you envisioned may need an update.

If you're searching for a budget school, look beyond the best-known names along the coasts such as New York University, Emerson, Santa Clara, Northeastern, Marymount, and American. These schools are expensive, and their financial aid packages are often poor. Look for colleges that are not situated in urban areas. There are great deals to be found in the Midwest, Mid-Atlantic, South, and Interior West.

Fortunately, there are lots of published analyses of colleges and universities that can help you evaluate your choices with data that allow you to compare universities with one another on a variety of measures. Junior may be scouring the list of party schools, but you should be checking out metrics such as per capita spending on education (instead of sushi and climbing walls), freshman retention (some schools, such as MIT, have high first-year dropout rates), and graduation rates (no six-year degrees). These statistics are published in

U.S. News & World Report's annual college rankings report. One of my favorite metrics is the return on investment (ROI) published by the *Princeton Review*. Just as businesses and investors consider ROI in choosing an investment, potential students should consider how well graduates of their favored institution perform in the real world, says the *Princeton Review*'s Rob Franek. Top ROI colleges include Harvey Mudd in Claremont, California, where grads earn median salaries of $73,300 out of the gate. Grads of Cooper Union for the Advancement of Science and Art in New York earn $61,300 on average. A lot of this advantage has to do with the field of study students at those institutions choose. Harvey Mudd is known for its science, engineering, and mathematics programs. In programs in which students study art, music, and design, starting salaries are significantly lower.

WHY YOU SHOULD FILE THE FAFSA

Once you have a short list of potential schools, you'll want to get a feel for how much free money you qualify for. The building blocks of a typical financial aid package are the following: federal need-based grants, work-study funding, and subsidized Stafford Loans. Subsidized means the government pays the interest on your loan while you are in college. Plus, there are merit-based scholarships offered by the institutions themselves. There are also unsubsidized federal loans and parent PLUS loans for Mom and Dad. The last of the list are private loans offered by banks. Generally, the farther you travel in this laundry list, the more you pay in interest and fees. Two-thirds of college students take out federal loans. For that reason, keep in mind that some are more advantageous than others. Exhaust federal loans first because they lock in the interest rates. Stafford is the best of the bunch. Your rate is locked in for the life of the loan but can be readjusted each summer for new borrowing. To be considered for any of these options, you have to fill out the Free Application for Federal Student Aid (FAFSA). Unbelievably, one study showed that *53 percent of eligible families did not bother applying for aid* through the FAFSA, leaving millions of dollars on the table. Many parents I talk to believe they aren't eligible for aid because they make too much money, but rising college costs have changed the equation. In fact, at current tuition levels, most families qualify for some type of aid.

Schools use the FAFSA to determine the gap between what a family can afford—called the expected family contribution (EFC), which I will talk about later—and the school's tuition. That's how schools determine whether a student should receive needs-based scholarships, or free money. To get the best results, start early, way early. According to Kal Chany, author of *Paying for College Without Going Broke*, parents should think about college planning the way they think about tax planning. He suggests applying for aid as early as when your child hits the ninth or tenth grade of high school to get a sense of how you fit in.

WAYS TO REDUCE YOUR EXPECTED
FAMILY CONTRIBUTION

Admissions lingo is full of jargon, but the most important term may well be your *expected family contribution*, which is what you are expected to pay. You don't decide this. As I said earlier in this chapter, the FAFSA is the tool schools use to determine the gap between what families can afford and a school's tuition. This is a number that savvy families manage just as surely as they manage their federal tax bill. The goal is to bring the number down, which in turn will increase the likelihood and size of any free money going to your future student. A good first step is *not* saving money in your child's name, but you can also take more dramatic steps to get more free money. Administrators scour your family's finances in the year you apply for admission, and typically that means a review of your finances from the tax season before. When you're under that spotlight, try to avoid any actions that could raise your income and therefore the amount of money administrators believe you have available to pay them. To do that, adjust your tax withholding to minimize refunds. Avoid early distributions from retirement plans. Some older parents may find they have to take a minimum distribution from an IRA. If you do, take *just* the minimum if you can. Minimize capital gains and don't cash in savings bonds in the years your income is being analyzed for student aid and loans (typically a year before you need the money). Some parents take college financial planning too far by turning down raises or even having a spouse quit his or her job. That is too extreme. Delaying a bonus into the next tax year makes sense, but turning down income does not. The goal is to minimize any discretionary income to maximize aid, not to make yourself poor.

Remember, the schools won't tell you how to position yourself for the most aid. You have to be savvy about the process. Your expected family contribution should help drive your college choice. If your expected contribution is high, you should search for schools that give merit scholarships to wealthy students. If your EFC is low, look for schools that are generous with financial aid.

It's not just parents who should be on the hook for financing a college education. Prospective students should contribute too. Working in college is a good way to discipline one's time. Another way students can help is by applying for scholarships. Some college counselors urge students to apply for every scholarship imaginable, hoping some obscure fund will pick up a big part of Johnny's costs. Truth is, lucrative scholarships attract thousands of applicants. A better option for many students is applying for smaller local scholarships awarded by community organizations such as a church or chamber of commerce. A free app to help you find scholarships that match your student is called ScholarshipAdvisor; it is available at the Apple iTunes app store.

Waiting for the acceptance letter and the financial aid package, which usually arrive in that order, is crunch time for Mom and Dad and the prospective student and typically a period of high anxiety. Most colleges will send out offers of admission anytime between March 1 and early April, and financial aid award letters arrive simultaneously or a few days later. The deadline for accepting offers of admission is typically May 1, what the schools call the National Decision Day. This gives you time to analyze offers and make comparisons between schools to get the best deal.

Some colleges have secure online portals they use to deliver the financial aid award letter instead of sending it by mail. Log in to the portal to check whether there are any messages waiting for you. Instructions may have been included with the admissions packet. If you are worried or if you have not received the financial aid award letter by mid-April, call the college's financial aid office to ask when you should expect to receive the letter. Some colleges will include this date in a financial aid time line on the college's website. After you receive the financial aid award letter, check whether you have to return a signed copy to the financial aid office. Some colleges require you to sign and return the letter within a week or two to accept the financial aid offer; others do not. The important thing here is to follow the rules. When it comes to college aid, deadlines matter.

Receiving the aid offer isn't the same as understanding it. The next step is decoding the details of the aid offer letter to determine how much money you'll be on the hook for, or your out-of-pocket costs. This sounds easy, but brace yourself. The letters are full of confusing jargon that is easily misinterpreted.

Consider an actual financial aid offer from Monmouth University in New Jersey that listed "alternative financing" of $8,865. Sounds like a handsome grant, right? It's not. It's a loan. Or consider the offer from the University of Arizona that included a "Wildcat T1" scholarship of $1,000. You've got to love free money, right? Nowhere does it say that the grant is only for the freshman year (*T* stands for "tuition reduction," and *1* stands for "freshman year"). Even worse are the letters that mislead parents about the full costs. In fact, fully a third of award letters don't even include the full cost of sending Junior to school. Yes, they include tuition and some fees, but major costs such as books, transportation, and living expenses are omitted or understated. That Monmouth University letter is instructive. It approximated total costs at $31,878, but in reality there was another $2,500 for travel and miscellaneous expenses and $900 for books that parents would have to contend with. The real cost was $35,000. The critical distinction you'll be making as you read the letter is whether the money the college is willing to give you is a grant, which does not have to be paid back, or a loan, which clearly does have to be paid back. You'd think it would be easy to discern this from the letter, but unfortunately it is not. Checking directly with the admissions office is typically the most reliable way to make sure you understand the specifics of the package. When you do, make sure you understand the following key pieces of information: cost of attendance, grants, scholarships, loans (both student loans and parent loans), work study, and expected family contribution.

Next you'll want to compare offers from different institutions. This is tricky, too, because the lingo that schools use is not standard among institutions. Some colleges call certain grants scholarships, which can be confused with government grants such as Pell Grants. You'll want to find the net cost to you. Know that the letters include a net cost figure, but that often includes loans. Beware of student loans masquerading as gift aid. To get an apples-to-apples comparison, you'll want to do the math on your own. Calculate a true cost of attendance and subtract grants, scholarships, and gift aid: money you will not have to pay back. Then compare these figures across institutions. One other caution: sometimes the very best aid package is given by the college in the freshman year to get a student in the door. In other words, the school may have no intention of repeating that lucrative package offered for the first year.

A free ride to college is a rare thing these days. If you are awaiting financial aid offers, you're hoping for a grant windfall, but the reality is that you will have to beef up your package with loans. Here's a list of the federal loans, their details, and their annual award limits.

FEDERAL PERKINS LOANS: These loans are available for undergraduate and graduate students. Eligibility depends on financial need and the availability of funds at the college. The college is the lender, and payment is owed to it. Undergraduates can get up to $5,500, and graduate students can get up to $8,000. Total amounts cannot exceed $27,500 for undergrads and $60,000 for graduate students.

DIRECT SUBSIDIZED LOANS: These loans are for undergraduate students who are enrolled at least half time and have demonstrated financial need. Interest isn't charged while the student is in school. The U.S. Department of Education is the lender, and payment is owed to it. Annual awards are $3,500 to $5,500.

DIRECT UNSUBSIDIZED LOANS: These loans are for undergraduate and graduate students who are enrolled at least half time. Financial need is not required. The student is responsible for paying interest throughout the life of the loan. Payment is owed to the Department of Education.

DIRECT PLUS LOANS: These loans are for the parents of dependent undergraduate students and for graduate or professional students. Financial need is not required. The student must be enrolled at least half time and must be either a dependent undergrad for whom a parent is taking out a Direct PLUS loan or a graduate or professional student who is receiving a Direct PLUS loan. The borrower cannot have a negative credit history and is responsible for paying interest in all periods. The Department of Education is the lender. The maximum award is the cost of attendance minus any other financial aid the student receives.

SPECIAL SITUATIONS

So many mothers and fathers these days are on second marriages (or even third) that I thought it was worth discussing what you need to know about your expected family contribution when things get a little complicated. First off, student aid officers have seen everything, so don't be shy or embarrassed. If Joanie's biological mom does not want to contribute to college costs, tell the aid officer that fact. However, what the schools *really* care about is not who the biological parents are but who a child's custodial parents are. What that means is that you must identify which parents the student lived with most in the year in which the institution is calculating your aid request. It's that parent or parents whose financial information will be used to determine your expected family contribution. Thus, even if you just remarried in the year aid is being calculated, the school will look at the assets and income of your new spouse as well as yours to determine your expected contribution. A stepmother or stepfather is treated as a natural parent by aid officers. If you're worried that a school will want to include your ex-spouse's massive Wall Street income in the aid calculation form, rest easy. The vast majority of colleges and universities never even ask to see information about the income or assets of a noncustodial parent.

Some business owners are also concerned about aid calculation. Here's what you need to know: for the most part, small-business or farm owners (defined as entities employing fewer than 101 full-time workers) don't have to report assets on the FAFSA form. This is a big change in the law that went into effect in 2006 that should supply relief to those who qualify. This means that your business equity, which is calculated as the value of the business minus its liabilities, doesn't have to be reported on the FAFSA and therefore won't increase your expected family contribution.

APPEALING THE AID OFFER

I n 2012, the average discount on tuition offered to incoming freshmen was 45 percent, an all-time high. Not everyone is offered that deal. What happens if you open the offer letter and are completely disappointed by the package from your dream school? One of the dirty little secrets of applying for the financial aid package is that you can appeal the school's decision. Thirty percent to 50 percent of families that ask for additional money from private colleges and universities get it. The first offer may not be the best and final one. School bureaucrats will be offended if you call it a negotiation, but most schools have guidelines for appealing for more aid. Find out what the rules are and follow them to the letter. This is no time for a sob story. If you have a true change in financial circumstances during the year, it's appropriate to ask for a new look at aid. Did Dad get laid off? Is Mom receiving expensive medical care? Include third-party documentation to support your case and include specific dollars amounts regarding any special circumstances. Remember, too, that many Ivy League schools will match needs-based offers from other schools. Any of these changes might cause a school to alter your aid package. Just don't call your efforts to increase aid a "negotiation" or ask for a "bargain." Instead, you want to "request a reconsideration of the aid that was offered."

Once your son or daughter has submitted an application, make sure the school understands the seriousness of your student's interest in attending. Now that students can apply to hundreds of schools with the click of a button, administrators don't want to waste their time working on an appeal for a student who will never attend.

A note to students considering applying for early admission: this will reduce your leverage on aid packages. Just 460 of the nearly 5,000 degree-granting institutions out there offer early admission, but they are some of the most popular and best-known colleges and universities, and their numbers are on the rise. For example, Stanford University boosted early admissions by a whopping 24 percent, and overall, early admissions are 7 percent higher.

Making early application means getting the process started the summer before senior year. Students who do this say they want to get in early to relieve the pressure of waiting for college acceptance letters with fellow classmates. According to some reports, admission rates are higher for early applicants than for those who follow the usual application deadlines, but critics say that applying early may benefit colleges and universities more than the students. Usually, applying early means you *must* accept a college's offer if it is made. For the school, that means locking in its pool of students early, and it gives the school an edge in the competition for the best students. But for high school seniors, it means less leverage at the negotiating tables when they are considering aid offers. It's difficult to make the case for more aid if you don't have any other offers to use as a bargaining chip with the student aid officer. If your college student is set on applying early, consider applying via "early action," which allows seniors to apply to multiple schools without committing to one institution.

JUGGLING THE TAX BENEFITS

The most important tax advice I can give parents who are applying for aid is that if you think there is any chance of getting financial aid, *don't put any money in your child's name.* Although many tax strategies call for families to do this, I say it's a mistake because federal aid assessment formulas will require that you put any money in your child's name to work—immediately. The name of the game is keeping control over your money. According to those formulas, typically 20 percent of your child's assets and 50 percent of the child's income will be assessed in determining how much the child can afford to pay for school. For parents, those levels are 47 percent of income and 5.65 percent of assets. In other words, federal rules would require a $2,260 payment from a $40,000 college fund held in the parents' name versus an $8,000 payment from a fund of the same size held in the child's name. At that rate, your college fund will be depleted fairly quickly.

I'm a big fan of the 529 college savings plan, but using it exclusively could lead you to lose out on some major tax benefits. Americans have saved more than $221 billion in these plans that operate like IRAs except that you never pay tax on the proceeds of your investments. That's the attraction of these plans. Your earnings grow while your child is in elementary and high school, and the distributions are tax-free if the money is used for qualified educational expenses such as tuition. But you can expand your savings dollars by using the following tax benefits. The first is the American Opportunity Tax Credit, which can reduce your tax bill by $2,500 for single filers making less than $80,000 and joint filers making less than $160,000. Remember, a tax credit, unlike a deduction, reduces your taxes dollar for dollar. The devil here is in the details. You won't be able to use the tax credit for room and board, though you can use it for tuition. (Use your 529 savings for room and board.)

Another tax benefit is worth noting, but be advised that it has lower income limitations. The Lifetime Learning Credit can reduce your tax bill by $2,000, but it's unavailable to single tax filers making more than $64,000 and joint filers making more than $128,000.

AVOIDING TROUBLED INSTITUTIONS

I mentioned earlier in this chapter that many of the college experts I tapped for information warned me that some colleges, especially private ones, may not be in business in another four years. It's hard to imagine that with the high price of tuition schools aren't luxuriating in massive budgets, but the truth is that a large proportion of colleges are financially stressed. The fact that a school is charging tuition and fees of $45,000 a year doesn't mean it is getting it. The problem got national attention in 2015 when Sweet Briar College, an all-women institution near Lynchburg, Virginia, announced it would close its doors. The 114-year-old liberal arts college that started as a finishing school cited "insurmountable financial challenges" as the reason for an abrupt announcement that it would close at the end of the academic year (it subsequently announced plans to reopen). Students were angry and sad. According to reports, the college had been discounting tuition by as much as 80 percent. But financial woes aren't limited to all-women colleges. Smaller schools have been merging with rivals for some time. Also, according to Moody's, a bond rating agency, operating revenue for four-year schools is on the decline. Its 2015 list of 18 "financially stressed" schools included well-known institutions such as Bard College in New York and Marymount University in Virginia. To be sure, the Moody's designation does not mean these schools will close tomorrow, but if you are looking for a school for your son or daughter to invest four years in, they are best avoided. Generally, the most troubled schools are ones that are smaller, are regional, and specialize in a narrow field of study. Getting your hands on a recent Moody's report can be difficult, and its list isn't complete as it follows only the top 500 schools. A better place for parents to check school financials is on the Department of Education's annual watch list found on its website at www.student aid.ed.gov. Here you can see a list of schools that have failed the department's financial responsibility test. Another warning sign is when a private school's average tuition discount is higher than 46 percent. Slashing prices demonstrates financial stress. Also ask whether the college is meeting its enrollment goals. Declining student body sizes also indicate trouble. Choosing a college or university is a decision that will affect your child for the rest of his or her life. The decision will affect not just the quality of children's education but what kinds of jobs they land and the professional relationships they form.

KEEPING COSTS DOWN DURING YOUR CHILD'S FOUR YEARS

It's easy enough for students busy with term papers and fraternity parties to lose track of how much debt they're racking up in college. After all, payments don't start until *after* graduation. For that reason, you'll want to stay focused on your student children's spending even if they aren't. This means careful choices from the beginning. Last year, the average cost of room and board was $9,800 (for the school year 2014–2015), but you can shave some money off that tab by choosing your dorm wisely. Housing that is right in the center of campus is more expensive than rooms that are on the periphery of the action, and a longer walk will mean Johnny may be spared that extra "freshman 10" pounds of weight gain. Food is a big expense for students because the options are so varied. Food trucks park along busy campus streets, offering tasty but expensive options, and the dining hall these days is no slouch. Students can get custom-designed meals. Chefs whip up breakfast omelets and French toast made to order. International cuisine is all the rage, and I'm not talking about a mushy taco. Chinese, Indian, and Greek options keep students from getting bored. This is all very nice, but it bumps up the costs for students. College meal plans are pricey. One smart option is to buy a reduced plan and eat breakfast in the room. After all, Mom and Dad don't eat breakfast out every day. At first blush, living off campus appears to be a far cheaper alternative. After all, splitting rent with roommates cuts your overall tab. But you'll have to be just as vigilant about costs that can spiral out of control. Be sure to consider the costs of utilities (especially Internet service), food, and transportation to and from campus. And don't forget to ask the landlord whether you can rent the place for 9 months rather than 12.

The only price rising faster than tuition is that of college textbooks. You can spend as much as $1,200 a year at a public college on textbooks and other supplemental materials required by professors, and some books cost as much as

$300 if you purchase them new. Fortunately, there are new solutions that will allow you to drive the prices lower. The most expensive place to buy books, new *and used,* is at the college bookstore. On Amazon.com, a $300 book was $110. Online is the best place to go for texts. Here's an example: An introductory psychology text recently cost $182 new and $136 used at the campus bookstore. On Amazon.com, the same book was $110. If you are buying online, use the ISBN number, a publisher identification code, to get the edition and title you're looking for. You don't have to limit yourself to Amazon and Barnes & Noble. Other good places to shop are AbeBooks.com and CengageBrain.com. CampusBooks .com will search multiple sites and help you find coupons or other deals. Those aren't the only options. Ebooks can be cheaper than the real thing, and a Kindle or another tablet is lighter to carry around campus. Plus, ebooks are searchable. Renting a book may be the best option for titles that a student will use in the current semester and never look at again. Savings can be as high as 80 percent. Many booksellers offer a rental option. Also check out Bookbyte.com, eCampus.com, and Chegg.com. As another option, free textbooks can be downloaded to your personal computer at OpenStaxCollege .com, which also offers print versions for $30 to $54. The books are peer-reviewed and best used for introductory texts, especially when the professor teaching the class hasn't authored his or her own text. Another option is buying an earlier edition of a textbook because the changes may not be substantial. In fact, in the example I gave of the psychology text, a previous edition of the paperback edition was available for just $4 online. By the way, there is always the college library for quick reads. If you're reading every book ever written by Jane Austen for a course, for example, you might want to take out some of them from the library. Remember that college libraries will borrow texts from other schools if they don't have a particular title on hand.

Another way to bring costs down is to get credit for courses that a student takes in high school. The way most students do this is through advanced placement (AP) curriculum and testing. Students sign up for advanced coursework in high school that is monitored and reviewed by the College Board, which administers and runs the SAT test for college admission. Students who take the coursework in high school can be granted college credits if they score well on AP tests. And that's not the only way to test out of college classes. Jay Cross, who founded doityourselfdegree.com, says virtually any student can ask to take a College Level Examination Program (CLEP) test by contacting the college itself. Costs are low: less than $100 in most cases. Cross used this strategy after realizing he needed another 30 credits to finish his bachelor's degree and finding the classes weren't being offered by the Connecticut college he was attending. He says the most compatible fields of study for testing out of classwork are business, accounting, psychology, and computer science.

Once you've settled on housing, bought the books, and decided on the meal plan, you'll have to consider how your child will handle out-of-pocket expenses. Credit card companies still hound students with card offers despite passage of the Credit CARD Act by Congress to discourage that practice. The law limited where card issuers could set up shop to market their wares, limiting them to more than 1,000 feet from campus or a school-related sporting event. The law also forbade these companies from handing out goodies such as gift cards and T-shirts. Trouble is, it seems card issuers have gotten smarter about promoting their wares. Beware! In my view, credit cards are kryptonite for students. Mom and Dad may think of it as an emergency get-out-of-jail-free card. A credit card, they rationalize, will allow their son or daughter to get out of a jam. Late getting back to campus from downtown? Take Uber. Need shoes or a shirt for the mixer? Put it on the card. You get the picture. A credit card may make Mom and Dad feel good, but for students it can be an easy way to lose any financial discipline. The average graduating student in 2013 faced $33,000 in debt from federal and state loans. The extra $3,000 that a graduating student owes in credit card debt doesn't sound like much, but it is debt your child could do without. Why add to the debt your children already are accruing? Remember, $3,000 is a mountain to a graduating senior who is facing an entry-level job and the costs of relocating and setting up a household.

A better way to encourage your children to manage their

expenses more actively *and* keep a close eye on what's going on is to load a prepaid debit card with a monthly allotment for spending money. If you are familiar with my reporting at all, you know I have been a frequent and harsh critic of debit cards because initially they were a feepalooza for the banks that issued them. They also made a heck of a lot of money for the celebrities who endorsed them, such as Justin Bieber and, inexplicably, the personal finance guru Suze Orman, who eventually pulled out after enduring a raft of criticism. But the world of debit cards has changed. Competition is increasing, and big national banks have gotten into the business, using lower fees as a lure. Find a bank that has ATMs and at least one brick-and-mortar office near the campus your student is attending. Check to make sure monthly maintenance fees are $3 or less and there is no charge for accessing funds at an ATM associated with the bank. Best case scenario: You use your current lender and set up a special account you can monitor separately. You put money into the account each month, and your son or daughter lives within that budget. That way, if they don't have enough money for going out to a movie at the end of the month, you and they know it's time to rethink spending. Keep in mind that the last thing you want is to give your child a debit or credit card linked to your existing account because that could create problems in paying your own monthly bills as well as confuse both of you. You want clear accountability for spending, not a mishmash of funds. Some parents say they want their sons and daughters to establish a credit history in their names by opening a credit card account. My response is that it is wiser to wait until they're employed full-time and can afford to pay the balance due.

KEEPING THE FAITH

It's daunting getting a child through college, yet every year nearly 2 million students are awarded bachelor's degrees. The truth is that American families are finding ways to make the seemingly impossible work. They are bringing down the cost of college and finding new sources for funding. My friend Patty, a single mom, just celebrated her son's graduation from MIT. Although she's far from wealthy, she didn't qualify for a single penny of aid. I asked her how she managed the tab, which totaled $150,000, on her own. "I scrimped on everything," she said. "There were no expensive vacations, no home renovations. I'm proud to say I made it myself."

Patty knows what so many parents of college students have come to realize. Choosing a college or university is a decision that will affect your children for the rest of their lives, determining not just the quality of their education but what kinds of jobs they land and professional relationships they form. The stakes are high, but determined parents can help their children make smart choices.

4

SURVIVING
OBAMACARE

Obamacare is pushing American families to take risks with their healthcare that the law's originators never imagined. Consider Rebecca, a hairdresser in a suburb of Dallas, Texas. The mother of three children ages 12, 14, and 16, Rebecca is self-employed. Her husband, a graphic arts designer, also works freelance. Together they earn $60,000 to $85,000 a year, depending on the strength of the local economy, and because they are self-employed, they have no health insurance from an employer. When Obamacare went into effect, requiring that the family get insurance coverage or pay a fine, Rebecca and her husband opted for the fine. Their analysis? Buying Obamacare coverage would cost them $700 a month in premiums, or $8,400 a year, which was higher than the Obamacare tax of 2 percent of their annual income, or $1,450. What's more, Rebecca's out-of-pocket cost for the family's healthcare was typically just $1,000 a year. Even with the fine, she judged they were still ahead financially. But then the worst happened. One of her children required surgery estimated to cost $22,000. Rebecca sprang to action and negotiated a better deal. She got the hospital to reduce her costs to just $4,000. "With no insurance, they slashed my prices dramatically because I self-pay," she said. "My family cannot be denied medical care, so I know we will be taken care of." Rebecca also knows that because she doesn't have coverage, she can go to virtually any hospital she needs. "I can go anywhere," she says.

Rebecca is one of millions of Americans who have opted out of the system. Although she is savvy about the healthcare system and uses its weaknesses to get the coverage she wants, the results, frankly, are not reliable. Patients simply cannot count on healthcare providers to discount their services. Yet there are some 35 million people still uninsured in this country who are making the same bet Rebecca is—that they can do better on their own than they can paying the hefty premiums and deductibles required by Obamacare. The irony is that Rebecca is doing exactly what Obamacare was designed to prevent, which is to say that she and her family are free riders on the system, taking services without paying for them. What is becoming increasingly clear is that the president's healthcare reform initiative isn't making affordable care broadly available; it's making healthcare unaffordable for many.

In this chapter, I'll help you and your family negotiate the confusing healthcare system that Obamacare ushered in. I'll show you how to read a medical bill and negotiate prices and arm you with the information you need to strong-arm providers. You'll learn how insurers "code up" your bill for maximum yield. I'll guide you through the process of controlling your costs and improving your care. Forced to find a new doctor because of insurance changes? I'll show you how to cross that Rubicon too.

To navigate this brave new world, however, you'll have to understand how Obamacare has changed the healthcare system. As Rebecca found, the most financially sound way of getting care may not be the most obvious. Unfortunately, five years after the Affordable Care Act was signed into law, many of us are still delaying care as a way to reduce our healthcare costs. In a recent poll, one-third of Americans said they or a family member delayed medical treatment because of the cost. That may mean opting for home remedies, cutting pills in half to save on prescription costs, or simply ignoring symptoms. That is happening because Obamacare is actually raising prices for healthcare consumers rather than lowering them. The promises of the president's signature healthcare legislation far outweigh the reality as the law enters its fifth year. One of the main selling points of Obamacare was that 46.3 million uninsured Americans would be guaranteed health coverage through the president's plan or their employers, Medicaid, or the Children's Health Insurance Program

(CHIP). Yet at year 5, more than 35 million Americans, like Rebecca, were still not insured. The president promised that Americans could keep their employer-sponsored plans, saying on 37 separate occasions that "if you like your healthcare plan, you can keep it." As the law went into effect in 2014, however, 4.7 million Americans lost their insurance coverage because their plans didn't meet the ACA's strict standards. Many of them were able to reenroll in new plans, but often with higher premiums in new provider networks that might or might not include their preferred caregivers. One of the great promises of Obamacare was that it would "bend the cost curve" and help "middle-class families." This is another goal that continues to elude the president. The average deductible for Obamacare coverage under the bronze plan was $5,081 in 2014, 42 percent higher than in comparable plans available to Americans using employee-sponsored coverage. When insurers began to file their plans for Obamacare coverage and costs for 2016, some asked for premium hikes of as much as 50 percent as they began to understand first-hand exactly what sorts of people they were insuring and what it would cost to give them coverage. Even the costs of working Americans who get insurance from employers is rising, although the rate of growth of those costs has slowed. According to the Kaiser Family Foundation, average annual premiums for employer-sponsored family health coverage were $16,834 in 2014, up 3 percent from the previous year. Deductibles in employer plans continued to rise as well.

Prices for policies in the individual market are rising as well, increasing 50 percent in 2014 as providers were forced to extend coverage to meet Obamacare's strict requirements.

The law's ballooning costs are largely the result of its failure to slow overall healthcare spending. Nationwide, health spending grew 5 percent in 2014, compared with 3.6 percent the year before, according to a report from the Altarum Institute. The Centers for Medicare & Medicaid Services forecast that spending would grow 6 percent per year between 2015 and 2023 largely as a result of the ACA's implementation. The president was adamant in promising that the Affordable Care Act would not add a dime to the deficit. I wish it were so. The reality is that the law was riddled with budget gimmicks that made it appear as if it paid for itself, but it does not. He originally claimed the plan would cost more than $900 billion over the next decade, but that price tag has ballooned to $1.2 trillion according to the Congressional Budget Office.

Has the law improved the quality of care? The answer is no, especially for seniors. The ACA made substantial cuts to Medicare to fund the law's subsidies for nonseniors on Obamacare, says Doug Holtz-Eakin, a former director of the Congressional Budget Office and president of the American Action Forum. Cuts to Medicare mean seniors will have less access to the doctors and care they need.

On every point, every promise, Obamacare has failed to deliver for Americans. What's more, the law has transformed the industry, which accounts for a fifth of total economic spending in this country, into a monolith even more unfriendly to consumers. In a world driven by complicated Obamacare rules and regulations, doctors are searching for cover. Many are finding welcome partners in hospital groups that are expanding their market share. Fewer doctors are willing to operate independently. They are taking down their sole-proprietor shingles and becoming employees. That increases the difficulty of getting the best care because when a doctor works in a government-run system, taking personal responsibility day to day is simply not rewarded as highly as is getting along and going along. If the experience at the Veterans Administration is any example, we could be in for real trouble. Statistics on the patient-doctor relationship offer little encouragement. Patients spend nearly twice as much time on average waiting for their doctors as actually talking to them. Once you get past the waiting room, the average doctor visit lasts just 10 to 15 minutes. Slender reimbursement rates mean the clock is ticking even before you sit down on the treatment table. And if you thought you'd find an eager listener to your healthcare concerns, think again. The average patient gets interrupted just 23 seconds into describing what his or her medical problem is—by the doctor, no less. The old Marcus Welby style of practice—sit, listen, evaluate—is long gone.

Insurers are running for cover as well. ACA nationalized the industry, allowing government to decide appropriate levels of profit for every company. Insurers that were in merger mode even before healthcare reform was signed into law are doubling down on the idea that bigger is better. In the state of Rhode Island, for example, Blue Cross & Blue Shield controls 95 percent of the market. The result of all this consolidation? Less choice and fewer options for consumers.

It's not just you against industry bean counters; it's also you against the government, which controls roughly half of healthcare spending in the country through programs such as Medicare, Medicaid, the Veterans Administration, and CHIP. Government bureaucrats' deep involvement in this industry results in erratic pricing. Want a Tylenol? If it's dispensed in a hospital, a single acetaminophen tablet could cost $1.50. For $1.49, you could get an entire bottle of the stuff at your local drugstore.

All this might be acceptable if the country could boast the best care in the world. Unfortunately, it can't. Among 17 high-income countries studied by the National Institutes of Health, the United States had the highest or nearly highest prevalence of infant mortality, heart and lung disease, sexually transmitted infections, and disability. The United States is at the bottom of the list for life expectancy. Men in this country live shorter lives—four fewer years—than do those in other wealthy developed nations. Yet we are paying more for care than are those in similar countries, an average of $8,402 per year per person. In other words, more spending, worse results.

HOW TO GET THE MOST OUT OF YOUR INSURER

Clearly, costs are continuing to rise for Americans, and behind the scenes doctors say they struggle to get reimbursed by insurers to cover their costs. A pediatrician at a major New York hospital told me the excuses she receives from insurers run from "We didn't receive your paperwork" to "You didn't fill out the paperwork correctly" to "You're not covered anyway." In fact, there is a war between insurers and doctors. Behind the scenes, an entire industry has grown up that advises medical offices on how to apply for reimbursement. Doctors spend hours learning about the complicated coding required by insurers to file a claim. There are seminars, newsletters, and even hacks describing these codes, which are called CPT (Current Procedural Codes) and are similar to SKU numbers on products in stores. File too aggressively and ask for too big a reimbursement, which is called "coding up," and the doctor's office is subject to fraud charges. Ask for too little and the doctor's costs aren't reimbursed.

Hospital groups are putting the pressure on doctors for savings by using "big data" to monitor doctors' work. The move is possible because of Obamacare requirements that patient data be made electronic. The upshot of these trends is that consumers are stuck in the middle and are being asked to foot a bigger proportion of their costs. "The insurers don't want to pay and hospitals and doctors do want to be paid, and the patients would like to have their services covered," says one surgeon.

Getting the best outcome, then, can be tricky. To get the best results, start by reading your insurance policy. No doubt it's boring, but reading it is the only way you'll know what you're covered for. If you have employer-sponsored coverage, you can get a copy of the policy from your human resources department. The details of ACA coverage also are available directly from insurers. If you are lucky enough to have your coverage provided by an employer, use that leverage to help get your bill paid. Your human resources department can run interference. Many large companies hire healthcare advocates who can help employees negotiate costs. If you are facing an expensive surgery or procedure, an advocate is paid a percentage of any settlement he or she gets for you. If you aren't in a corporate plan, you can independently hire an advocate to take your case. At a minimum, a healthcare advocate can review your bill and your situation, looking for errors and getting the bill adjusted on the basis of his or her knowledge of competitive rates. Some people hire healthcare advocates to manage all their healthcare needs, including booking appointments and managing bills. The truth is that any three people can walk into a doctor's office with the same problem and be charged different amounts.

To get the most out of your insurer, you need to

understand deductibles. Eighty percent of workers with employer-provided health coverage pay a deductible, an out-of-pocket payment made by employees, before their coverage kicks in. In 2014, the average deductible was $1,217, up 47 percent from $826 five years earlier, according to Kaiser. The amount you pay out of pocket before your insurer starts picking up the tab can be confusing. Even if you pay the entire bill from a doctor for a service or test, the full payment may not be applied to your deductible. An insurer may credit you for less, say, the costs that Medicare would reimburse plus 10 percent. Let's say you run up a $250 bill for an exam from your primary care physician. An insurer may credit you for the amount Medicare would reimburse the doctor for a similar service, say, $80, plus another 10 percent, or $88, rather than the $250 you paid. You also may find that you have multiple deductibles, one for medications, another for your provider's treatments, and yet another for hospital treatments.

SHOPPING AROUND FOR THE BEST POLICY

Typically, every fall, employers offer their workers options when it comes to healthcare coverage. Don't let your insurance renewals go on autopilot without first understanding any changes in coverage and costs. If you have coverage under ACA, make sure you understand whether you will be automatically renewed in the same policy you had last year.

Be sure to compare both monthly premiums and deductibles to get an apples-to-apples comparison of your total costs. Inside or outside Obamacare, healthcare insurers change their policies every year. One way to save money is to use a health savings account. On average, the cost of coverage associated with a health savings account is 20 percent less than that of a plan structured as a health maintenance organization. That's the case because many employers make contributions to a health savings account (HSA) on your behalf and the money is yours to keep even if you switch jobs. HSAs offer a triple tax advantage. Tax-free contributions generate tax-free interest that can accumulate until retirement and be used tax-free for medical expenses. Contributions are limited to $3,350 per year for individuals and $6,650 for couples. Some employers offer flexible savings accounts (FSAs), which allow an employee to set aside pretax dollars to pay for certain medical expenses and some dependent care expenses. Limits for contributions are $2,550, and some require you to use the money or lose it, unlike HSAs, which are more like 401(k)s. The trick to managing an FSA effectively is to submit all your eligible expenses, deductibles, copayments, and coinsurance costs not reimbursed by insurance. Check your balance well before the annual December 31 deadline to be sure you use all your money. It also pays to evaluate your spending from year to year to make sure you set aside enough dollars to cover routine costs.

One of the negatives of Obamacare is that it has encouraged insurers to offer fewer doctors and fewer hospital options to consumers, a phenomenon health experts call narrow networks. About 50 percent of ACA plans and almost 25 percent of employer-based plans are narrow network plans that may include only a third to half of the largest hospitals in their network and a similarly small number of doctors and specialists. As you shop around, be sure that the doctors and facilities you need are in your plan. Getting care that is out of network will cost you (I will explain in a moment). There's only one source of funds for doctors who are not in your insurance network, and that's your pocketbook.

WHEN YOU SHOULD CHANGE DOCTORS

People spend more time researching and buying a car or choosing furniture than they do picking a primary care physician, according to the American Institute for Preventive Medicine. Not only do consumers do little due diligence in choosing a doctor, they are unlikely to change doctors voluntarily. Many people are reluctant to switch even if a doctor is no longer in their network. They're nervous about offending the doctor and reluctant to dump a physician who knows their history. But here is the new reality: as insurance companies consolidate and networks change, being forced to find a new doctor is much more likely. What's more, as you change and age, the doctor you originally chose to serve your family may not be the right fit anymore. That said, choosing a new doctor isn't easy. In fact, with some 850,000 doctors out there, it can be overwhelming trying to find the right match for you.

Here are the key factors to picking the best physician: Start your list with the doctors who are in your insurance network. Picking a physician outside your network is a recipe for financial disaster, because you probably will end up picking up most of the bill for every single visit even if you are simply getting a flu shot. If you figure that the average cost per visit is $200 and the average family of four goes to the doctor's office 16 times a year, you could be facing a hefty $3,200 tab every year. It is much better to make the average $22 copayment.

Solicit advice from friends and family. Often, those closest to you have experience with local doctors. Ask them the questions that are difficult to answer: Is their doctor responsive? Do you spend hours waiting to see him or her? Ask whether the doctor is a good listener; remember, the average physician interrupts his or her patients just 23 seconds into their description of their ailments. Does your physician take questions by e-mail? How nice is the office staff? When you're sick and seeking care, all these issues take on greater importance.

Find out your doctor's credentials. Credentials matter, and many of them have to be updated periodically. A gynecologist, for example, has to pass a written and oral certification every six years with the American Board of Obstetrics and Gynecology. Your insurer's website may give you basic information on the educational and professional backgrounds of its member physicians. If it does not, check out these organizations: Administrators in Medicine (DocBoard.org) provides information on licensing and disciplinary actions for doctors in 18 states, and the American Medical Association's DoctorFinder (https://extapps.ama-assn.org/doctorfinder) has comprehensive information on member doctors, including their educational backgrounds and areas of specialization.

Check out online patient reviews as well. Sites such as HealthGrades.com and Vitals.com rank doctors on the basis of patient reviews.

HOW TO DECIPHER YOUR MEDICAL BILL

There was a time not that long ago when a patient might never see a medical bill, much less have to read it. However, few of us can afford to be blissfully ignorant anymore as rising costs force insurers and employers to push higher deductibles and co-pays onto consumers.

What's worse, when you get your bill, you may realize it's written in a language you don't understand. Bills are full of complex coding and shorthand that I think insiders hope you never really understand. That strategy is working so far. Fully 77 percent of Americans say they don't understand either the medical bills they receive or their health insurance. But it pays to be persistent. According to Medical Billing Advocates of America, 80 percent of medical bills contain an error. The most common ones are duplicate billing, typos in which the wrong coding or price is entered, charges for work that was canceled, and inflated operating room fees. These errors could be in your favor. Either way, it pays to know if your bill is wrong.

Charges can come from a variety of different sources, such as your doctor for the exam, the lab for testing, and maybe radiology for x-ray services. The list can go on and on. With different sources the possibilities for mistakes and errors escalate.

The second thing you'll notice on an itemized bill from your doctor or hospital is the five-figure codes. These are the CPT codes we discussed earlier in this chapter. They are assigned to each and every service a primary care physician, specialist, or technician provides to a patient, including medical, surgical, and diagnostic services. You can look up what these codes mean by going to the American Medical Association's CodeManager on its website (https://ocm

.ama-assn.org/OCM/CPTRelativeValueSearch.do). You'll have to fill out some details about yourself and promise not to use the information for anything but your personal use, but going to this extra trouble will allow you to see precisely what you are being billed for. That said, remember that some healthcare workers spend their entire careers mastering the CPT codes, so if you're having trouble understanding them, ask your doctor's office for details.

The story of what you pay doesn't end with the doctor's bill. You'll also receive an EOB (explanation of benefits), from your insurer or Medicare. It will show how much of each service was paid for on your behalf. As on the doctor's bill, each service is coded. You'll want to verify that the CPT codes on your doctor's statement match the codes on the insurer's statement to be sure that you're being charged for the services you are receiving. If they don't match, contact your doctor and the insurance company.

The bottom line? At the bottom of your final bill, you'll see a line item called the charge. Consider this the sticker price, not the final price. The discounted price, or adjustment, will follow, which will factor in anything you've already paid from your co-pay. The balance (sometimes called the patient responsibility) is your final bill with whatever late fees or credits have accrued.

HOW TO LOWER YOUR BILL

When Dr. Jeff Rice, a Nashville radiologist, was looking for a hospital for his son's foot surgery, he was surprised to find a huge disparity in prices. The first institution he contacted said the price would be $15,000. Surprised, he started to shop around and contacted other surgeons he knew were good at other facilities. Just three blocks away at another hospital, he was quoted a price of $1,500—a tenth of the first price. Don't be surprised; such inequalities are common. Rice had no regrets about choosing the cheaper institution and doctor. His son's recovery went as scheduled, and it all worked out just as he hoped. The differences in prices, he says, don't necessarily speak to the quality of care. Instead, they are the result of the prices that different insurers are able to negotiate with providers. Many other factors can come into play, such as whether the hospital you choose is a teaching hospital or takes on a lot of uninsured patients. One of the biggest factors in terms of the cost is your insurer's ability to drive down costs. It was that experience that caused Rice to start Healthcare Bluebook (HealthcareBluebook.com), where people can find out the average cost of procedures, tests, and surgeries all over the country. By simply filling in your Zip Code, you can access Rice's impressive database, which can guide you in learning whether you're getting a fair price.

Getting that fair price, though, will require you to

negotiate, and that can be easier said than done. To negotiate your bill effectively, you'll need facts. In the New York City area, prices for a colonoscopy can range from $2,000 to $25,000. The differences in those tests? Not a thing. Go to HealthcareBluebook.com or NewChoiceHealth.com to compare prices on everything from drugs to surgeries. In this case, knowledge is power. In the best-case scenario, you'll negotiate prices before receiving treatment. Once you have had the service or procedure, it's much harder to negotiate prices because a bill is considered a legal document in the healthcare industry. Thus, *when* you negotiate is as important as how you negotiate. Offering a doctor or hospital speedy payment—say, before the billing even occurs—can net you as much as 50 percent in savings. In contrast, it's more difficult to get the hospital and the staff in the hospital's billing center to lower prices that already have been entered into the system. That is doubly true for uninsured patients. One community hospital board member said government billing practices encourage hospitals to boost the cost of services to patients with no insurance by as much as half. By simply calling and asking for a price reduction, those who are uninsured can net big savings, he said.

Be sure to document any doctor visits. Trips to the hospital are often stressful and time-consuming. It's likely that you won't pay attention to all the medical details about what procedures you're going to get, but that's where you can save money: by paying attention! While you're at your doctor's office, take notes or have a family member take notes about which doctors came to visit and when, what tests were ordered, and what supplies were used. Then ask for an itemized statement when you leave. Again, billing errors are common because the staff often fills in an incorrect coding number or types that number in duplicate. Then review your bill. Here's where the pedal hits the metal. Compare your notes from your visit with the itemized statement and the final bill that has been through the insurers' offices. You may already have caught discrepancies between the itemized statement and your notes from the doctor's visit. Look for any discrepancy between the doctor's bill and that of the insurer. If you feel there are miscellaneous charges or the bill is too expensive, contact the hospital's billing department for an explanation as well as your insurer to see what you are covered for. If all else fails, call in the experts. Negotiating medical bills is tricky business, especially for a complicated and expensive operation or procedure. Many consumers turn to professional advocates such as MedicalCostAdvocate .com and BillAdvocates.com to get bills lowered. Medical billing advocates are familiar with hospital and insurer systems. They also have a relationship with people inside the healthcare establishment and usually can contact the right people, which can be difficult for those of us who are not part of the healthcare system. The services are not free. Most billing advocates charge 35 percent of the reduced price if their negotiating is successful; others charge an hourly fee. Keep in mind that if they are unable to get your bill lowered, they should charge you nothing at all. Ask about the charges up front.

LOWERING DRUG COSTS

Half of all Americans take a prescription drug regularly, spending a collective $374 billion in 2014 for a range of drugs, everything from blood thinners to painkillers. The thing your pharmacist won't tell you is that the price for your prescription allergy meds may be higher than the price of the same prescription drug at a different pharmacy down the street. You may assume that the price is the same everywhere, but it is not. Fortunately, an app called GoodRx can help you compare prices at drugstores in your area. Check out drug coupons at RxRevu.com or go to a legitimate online pharmacy to shave 35 percent or more off the cost of your medication. Keep in mind that pharmaceutical companies offer patient assistance programs for those who can't afford their medications. Another way to save is to use over-the-counter remedies for conditions that aren't life-threatening, such as seasonal allergies, heartburn, and insomnia.

Another hidden secret of the healthcare industry: the expiration date on your prescription or over-the-counter medications may be virtually meaningless. An expiration date is required by the federal government and some state governments, but drug experts say that with only a few exceptions there is very little science to prove that drugs are less effective or dangerous when used beyond the expiration date. In fact, most drugs aren't even tested for shelf life. One of the rare studies conducted found that 88 percent of drugs could be used past the expiration date for a period of 66 months, or five and a half years. Some drugs can last even longer. According to the Federal Drug Administration (FDA), users of amoxicillin, ciprofloxacin, and diphenhydramine can extend the shelf life of their drugs anywhere from 1 to 15 years. There is one exception: tetracycline, an antibiotic that can become toxic if used after its expiration date. To extend the life of your drugs, move them out of the medicine cabinet, where humidity can hurt their effectiveness. If you're nervous about whether an expired prescription is still safe, stick to the sell-by dates on drugs you absolutely must have, such as an EpiPen or heart medications, and keep nonprescription drugs such as aspirin on the shelf longer.

CONCLUSION

In sum, getting heathcare at a reasonable price is not a simple endeavor in today's world. Obamacare has made dramatic changes in the structure of the industry, and costs continue to rise. More and more of those costs are being passed on to and paid for by working Americans. To get the best solution for your health and your wallet, understand what you are paying so that you can go elsewhere if necessary. Increasingly, doctors and hospitals are on the hook for providing fair prices to consumers. By having information about relative prices in your area of the country, you can hold their feet to the fire.

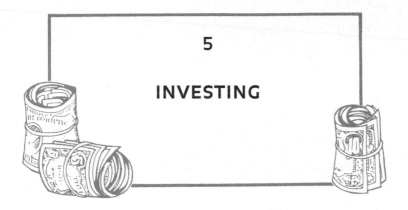

5

INVESTING

Back when the whole world seemed to be coming to an end during the financial crisis in 2008, a close friend called me. He sounded both defiant and relieved. He said he had pulled all his retirement savings out of every investment he had. Stocks had been sold, and bond funds liquidated. He had put this cash into a money market fund. "The whole thing's rigged!" he exclaimed. "I can't deal with the anxiety." And there his money sat for four years, losing value against inflation even as one of the biggest bull markets of the last 58 years got under way. And he's not alone. Plenty of people have done exactly the same thing. The American public has lost faith in investing as a way of preparing for the future. Fewer and fewer of us invest in stocks. Ownership of individual stocks has dwindled to 13.8 percent of the population, down from 21.2 percent in 2001. Fewer of us own stocks in our 401(k)s. Just 48 percent of us own stock funds, compared with 53 percent in 2007. The reasons? When surveyed by Bankrate.com, people cited three big reasons for staying away. First, they said they simply lacked the money. That's understandable in light of the economic malaise we've been experiencing. Reason number two was lack of knowledge, and reason number three was that they didn't trust brokers or advisers. This chapter will address those concerns. I'll show you exactly what you are up against as an investor: the poor Obama policies and Wall Street practices that make for a playing field that gives the advantage to insiders. Then we'll look at how you can fight back and earn the retirement you deserve.

It's not just the experience of the deepest bear market since the Great Depression that has people worried. The way the financial markets work doesn't inspire much confidence. Take, for example, Bernie Madoff, a Manhattan financial adviser who counseled families in some of the most elite social circles in Manhattan. His entire business was nothing more than a Ponzi scheme. Instead of investing clients' money, he stole it for his own purposes, defrauding them of billions. The scheme, once exposed, shook financial circles because of Madoff's high profile. He was arrested in his Upper East Side penthouse apartment after finally admitting to family members that his business was a fraud, and he was sentenced to 150 years in jail in June 2009. The judged termed his fraud "extraordinarily evil."

Wall Street practices aren't doing much to encourage small investors. The very way in which stocks are traded has come into question as superfast sophisticated computers allow some traders to manipulate the market and extract billions in profits. The flash crash of 2010, when stocks temporarily plunged 1,000 points in a single day, shocked investors, traders, and regulators. Nearly $1 trillion of value was erased temporarily as shares of some companies plummeted to pennies on the dollar. For small investors, the question inevitably is, What if my trade ended up in the middle of something like the flash crash? Regulators ultimately blamed a British trader for setting the minicrash into motion by using complex trading programs to trick investors into thinking the market was moving in a particular direction and then exploiting that misinformation, a practice known as spoofing. They say the trader made a total of $49 million in profits by using those techniques.

Unfortunately, the May 6, 2010, flash crash wasn't the only crash of that type, and even today smaller flash crashes occur frequently. Superfast trading similar to the sort used by the British trader is common on Wall Street. High-frequency traders flood the market with orders and then pull the vast majority of them back, testing the waters for sentiment and acting on that information. They go so far as to locate their operations close to exchanges to shave milliseconds off their response time. If all this seems confusing or troubling, I don't blame you. To be sure, rogue advisers like Madoff are not uncommon, but if you're smart and not too greedy you can avoid them. However, the changes in the way Wall Street traders make their money should make all of us cautious. Trading frequently exposes you to more risk than does simply buying and holding. Read on and I will describe how small investors can do well by not doing too much. One thing I wish regulators and market regulars would realize, however, is that these new trading practices have unnerved many small investors. We are pulling out of the market in record numbers, and that's not good for anyone because investors, including small investors, are the lifeblood of the economy. We provide the capital that spurs job creation, innovation, and entrepreneurship. The equity markets should be a place where small investors are treated fairly and with respect.

All of this, however, does *not* mean you should abandon the stock market, because the fact is that the stock market, even today, offers better returns than does any other asset class—*over time.* In other words, if you don't have time to allow your money to percolate for at least 5 years and possibly 10, sit out the stock market. But if you do have that time, you need to get in. Sitting on your hands because you're worried about a handful of high-frequency traders and cheaters on Wall Street means you are missing the forest for the trees. Remember, individuals shouldn't be jumping in and out of the market anyway. You should be putting money in slowly, over time. By doing that, you limit your exposure to market breaks such as a flash crash, a sudden up and down driven by unforeseen events. No doubt that *is* gut-wrenching. My friend who pulled out of the market in 2008 missed out on years of gains. Yes, the S&P fell 36.55 percent, and that was gut-wrenching, but in 2009 the S&P 500 rose 25.94 percent, and in 2010 it was up another 14.82 percent. In a single year, 2013, the S&P 500 catapulted 32.15 percent. Get the picture? The market is cyclical. It has ups and downs, and if you bail because of a bad year, you set yourself up for missing gains in the good years that are sure to follow. According to Wharton professor Jeremy Siegel, the compound annual return from stocks is 6.6 percent over the long haul. In my view, if you want to be financially successful, you have to invest in the stock market.

That said, I wish I could say the federal government is trying to help us in our quest to build retirement savings. After all, isn't it in Washington's interest to keep us less dependent on government handouts in our retirement? You wouldn't think so from Obama's initiatives in this arena. Despite overwhelming evidence that Americans are undersaved for retirement—a BlackRock survey shows that 4 in 10 Americans haven't even started saving for retirement—Obama's administration is focused like a laser on raising tax revenues even if it means discouraging us from setting aside money for retirement. The president has proposed limiting retirement account balances to $3 million, an amount that would fund an annuity paying little more than $200,000 a year. Who is the federal government to tell us how much we will need in retirement? The feds may believe $3 million is the most you should be allowed to save in a 401(k) account after a lifetime of sacrifice and hard work, but that is roughly the value of a California police sergeant's pension if he or she works for 30 years, retires at 50, and lives a normal life expectancy, according to the *Wall Street Journal*. The federal government should be encouraging us to funnel money into our retirement savings, not finding new ways to limit their use. Private savings supplement federal safety-net programs such as Social Security by helping millions of us prepare for the future. Encouraging savings could ultimately reduce the burden on the federal government of supporting Americans in retirement. Obama's programs suggest that Americans have too much money in tax-sheltered savings for retirement. In fact, the opposite is true. The National Institute on Retirement Security reported that 40 million American households have no retirement savings at all and that the median account balance for those of us who are saving is just $2,500. The problem, quite obviously, isn't that we are *oversaving* for retirement; it's quite the opposite. I believe the federal government should be encouraging retirement savings and investment, not discouraging them by putting in caps.

Other programs suggested by the Obama administration to deal with the lack of retirement savings, such as myRA, are similarly misguided. This program was developed as a starter vehicle to encourage the middle class, especially young people, to save for retirement, and the idea behind it, according to the White House, was to develop a "simple, safe and secure" investment option. Minimum investments are set low—just $25—and can be taken out any time. But the myRA program offers just one investment option to investors, a "savings bond like" investment that would mimic the return that government employees get in their retirement accounts. Over the last five years, those returns have averaged just 2.69 percent a year, well below the returns from the stock market. One analysis of the myRA plan estimated that it would take an investor contributing $50 every two weeks 11 years to amass $15,000. That's not investing; it's more like a rainy day passbook savings account. With returns so low and investment options so few, this is a dreadful deal for small investors. Americans are reluctant to invest in their 401(k)s even when they get matching employer dollars. Participation rates are just 53 percent except when employers automatically enroll workers. Young investors *do* need to start saving for retirement, but they should experience the real world of investing, where risk and reward go hand in hand. Obama also wanted to impose mandatory minimum distributions on Roth IRAs, just like regular IRAs. Required minimum distributions (RMDs) are a terrible deal for investors; expanding their use is simply bad policy. I'll tell you more about this later in this chapter as we dive into the best way to invest for the long term.

My theory of investing is simple: invest all the time.

When stocks are up, invest. When stocks are down, invest. Unfortunately, most people want to yank their money out of the market when stocks are falling. But think about it: if you continue investing when prices are falling, you'll lower your overall costs of investing. Even the best companies' shares fall in a bear market. If anything, you should slow down on investing new dollars when prices are *high*, not low. But this idea confounds small investors. Instead, they follow their gut, react to fear, and make poor decisions.

Another secret that the pros know that you may not is how valuable a commodity *time* is in growing investments. One of the first lessons business school students learn is what is called the time value of money. I learned this at Columbia University's business school. All the phrase means is that a dollar you earn today is worth more than a dollar you earn tomorrow because of the simple fact that you can invest today's dollar, earning money on your money. Benjamin Franklin had it right. Time, in fact, *is* money. That essentially is the power of compounding. When you save and invest regularly—even small amounts—you grow your money far more quickly than you do when you wait until later to invest. For example, imagine a 20-year-old woman who makes a one-time contribution of $5,000 to her IRA and earns an annual average return of 8 percent. Over her working life of 45 years, her one-time investment will grow to nearly $180,000. That's without sweetening the pot, without adding one dollar. Imagine, however, if she had added

$5,000 a year *every year* over the same stretch of time, earning the same return. Her savings would have grown to more than $2 million! The secret is allowing time for your money to grow *as well as* adding money to the pot. Regular investing at periodic intervals is the key. The rule of 72 demonstrates the power of compounding. Let's say you have seven years until you want to retire and feel you need to double your retirement savings to be fully prepared. Take 72 and divide it by 7. It tells you you'll need to get a return of 10.3 percent per year to achieve your goal. This exercise allows you to test your expectations against the real world. Let's say your returns are more modest. Maybe you're earning 4 percent on your money each year right now. Using the rule of 72, it would take you 18 years to double your money (72 divided by 4).

All right, you've read my money basics lecture and may be thinking to yourself, Gerri, I do all this, and I still never get the returns of the broader market. Truth is, it may feel that way at times. In fact, when retirement account balances set a record high in 2014 at $91,300, the average was just 2 percent over the previous year's balances despite the fact that the market was up 13.5 percent that year. In fact, 33 percent of investors ended up with negative or zero returns that year. Why? Few investors were 100 percent invested in the markets in 2014. Your results won't track market performance perfectly because retirement experts suggest that you should have a balanced portfolio that will include more than just

U.S. stocks to reduce the impact of a downturn in the markets on your portfolio. I'll cover asset allocation a little later, but before we leave this topic I want to point out that if you're disappointed with *your* returns over the last few years, you should see what's happened to hedge fund operators, advisers to the superwealthy who are supposed to have great performance to earn their hefty commissions. Those managers have consistently underperformed the markets. Next, I want to get down to the nitty-gritty. I am going to define terms we use every day to make sure you understand the investing products and tools you will be using or are using now. Then, we'll talk about managing your investments over time and how to tap them in retirement. I'll address when you should seek professional advice and when you should go it alone.

DECIDING WHETHER TO INVEST
IN INDIVIDUAL STOCKS

Personally, I don't invest in individual stocks. I don't have time to do the research it takes to pick stocks and manage them over time. This is where insiders have a real advantage in terms of information. Hedge fund managers and other investing professionals spend a small fortune on data that I can't match. Timely and critical information is key. Not only can I not afford a Bloomberg terminal in my office, I don't have time to analyze every bit of information that is produced by the thousands of folks selling market and stock data. Some investors don't look for the needle in the haystack but instead buy and hold what they consider blue chip stocks. Many of our parents bought Ford, GM, GE, and the like. Some of my friends think of Apple as the GE of today's generation. Although Apple has been an impressive company with an incomparable product line over the last 10 years, the tech industry is notoriously fickle. Today's Apple watch may be tomorrow's Walkman. More to the point, putting the kids' college fund in a single company's shares, even Apple shares, in my view would be foolish. If you pick the wrong stock—and there are plenty of wrong stocks—you could not only not make money on your investment but actually lose money. The idea that a special class of stocks grows to the sky was largely disproved in the last stock market crash, when all stocks lost value. If you want to invest in individual stocks, fine, go for it. But do it with your vacation money, not your retirement fund or the kids' college fund. For my money, I believe there is safety in numbers. In other words, I'd prefer to invest in a larger portfolio in which I can get more diversification; my returns may be lower, but my risk is less. If one or two or more stocks go down in value, that is offset by the growth of the other stocks in the portfolio. This leads me to mutual funds.

THE ROLE OF MUTUAL FUNDS IN
YOUR RETIREMENT ACCOUNT

People think that being successful financially is about having access to the high-risk, high-reward investments used by Wall Street insiders. The truth is that those high-flying investments crash and burn as much as they soar. You don't have to have access to Wall Street's latest best idea to be successful over time. For most of us, mutual funds are the easiest to use and the most flexible investments. Many people have no idea what a fund is or what they actually own when they buy one. A mutual fund is a company that pools money from many investors to invest in stocks, bonds, or other assets. Its combined holdings are called its portfolio. Each mutual fund share represents an investor's proportionate ownership of the fund's holdings and the income it generates. You don't own the stocks or bonds the funds invest in; what you own is a share of the fund, which you can buy from the fund company or from a broker. One big advantage is that a mutual fund offers small investors access to professionally managed portfolios and a diversity that normally would require much more capital to achieve. A mutual fund makes money for you through capital gains distributions or dividend payments, or it may increase its NAV (net asset value), its price per share, which rises with a rise in the investments it holds. Another option is investing in exchange-traded funds (ETFs), which have the advantage over mutual funds of having lower costs for the most part as well as trading like a stock, which means you can get into and out of an investment easily. A warning here, though: in the August 2015 market sell-off, some ETFs were priced incorrectly at a time of panic selling. Individual investors were hurt. Therefore, buy ETFs for the price advantage but don't count on selling in a market panic.

THE AVERAGE 401(k) investor has the option of investing in 25 different funds, but in the wider financial world there are a bewildering total of more than 7,000 different mutual funds. Also, fund investors are well advised to watch the fees they pay to the managers of the fund, which can be tricky. High fees can have a significant impact on your net returns.

MUTUAL FUND FEES: When you are analyzing fees, the first number you want to look for is a mutual fund's *expense ratio*. That's the annual percentage of your money that the fund company charges to manage the fund. You pay this over time, each and every year. The money goes to pay the fund manager's salary, which is no small thing. Even the smallest fund, say, one with $250 million in assets, may pay an active manager 0.5 percent, or $1.25 million—not a bad salary! Also included in the number are administrative costs such as postage, record keeping, and customer service. Then there are the marketing costs, or the 12b-1 fee. Yes, you pay for advertising the fund. You may also be charged a "load," or sales charge on purchases. The pros call the fee for getting into a fund a front-end load. The fees go to brokers for selling the fund and generally can be avoided. Likewise, some funds also carry a back-end load or contingent deferred sales load, a fee that goes straight in the broker's pocket. You can side-step this one too. Even small numbers add up. A 1 percent expense ratio means the fund keeps $1 for every $100 you have invested with it, every year. Actively managed funds can charge an average of 1.12 percent. Index funds (see below), which require far less maintenance, charge far less. The Vanguard Total Stock Market Admiral Shares fund has an expense ratio of 0.06 percent. The difference may look small, but over time these differences add up. The bottom line is this: fees are critical. Whatever you choose to pay the mutual fund company for running the fund or a broker for selling it to you comes right out of your return. Nor do higher fees make for better performance. In fact, the opposite can be true.

ACTIVE OR PASSIVELY MANAGED FUNDS: This topic is the subject of incredibly intense debates. Advocates of index funds, in which there is no stock selection and the fund simply tracks a benchmark such as the S&P 500, say the lower costs are critical to getting the best performance over time. They say active managers can't keep up with their benchmarks, much less beat them. To be sure, over the last few years of the bull market, active managers have been hard pressed to keep up with the averages. Just 26 percent of domestic stock fund managers were able to deliver higher returns than their benchmark over a five-year period ending in June 2014. Even worse, 87 percent of large-cap stock fund managers failed to beat the S&P 500 during that time. As a result, investors headed for the exit, pulling out $70 billion in 2014. But markets aren't always rocketing to the sky. I believe there is a season for both varieties of funds. When it comes to owning large-cap U.S. stocks, I invest in an ETF that tracks the S&P 500 because I believe that's the most efficient way to invest. But there are markets in which active managers can add value, such as municipal bonds and some international markets. Index investing has been in favor in recent years because the markets have had enormous returns, but it won't always be that way. If you do opt to use an active manager, choose one that has relatively low trading costs. Excessive trading can be a drag on your retirement.

MANAGING YOUR INVESTMENTS
INTELLIGENTLY OVER TIME

There are two kinds of investors in my view. There are people who jump in and out of investments, raising their costs as they follow the next big trend. They may keep a substantial portion of their pool of money in cash to allow them to take advantage of opportunities. Then there are people who choose an asset allocation that fits their age and time of life. They pick the funds best suited for them and then invest over time, slowly and consistently. I am the latter type. Even during 2008, when the S&P 500 lost 36 percent of its value, I kept my investments active and continued investing every single month. Yes, I lost 30 percent of my retirement portfolio in that sell-off. But then I turned around and bought at much lower prices as the markets soared, going up 25.9 percent in 2009 and even more in 2013. Not only has my portfolio recovered, it has made impressive gains. In my view, the way you manage your money over time is as important as what you invest in. To make the most of the advice I've given you, you'll need to get the best asset allocation possible. Websites such as those of Betterment, Vanguard, and Morningstar, as well as your own financial adviser if you are using one, can help you figure out what proproportion of your savings to allocate to domestic stocks, international equities, and bonds. A typical mix is 60 percent stocks and 40 percent bonds for investors who are decades from retirement. Over time, the allocations switch so that more money is in less risky bonds, but it depends on your personal circumstances. Next, you'll need to manage this mix over time. When stocks are soaring, as they have in recent years, you'll find that the stock portion of your portfolio grows like Topsy. You'll want to rebalance that portfolio to bring the allocations into line at least once a year. That may mean selling some stock investments to bolster another part of your portfolio. This may sound like a small thing, but over time it matters, just like trimming your hedges. The differences may not be large from year to year, but as the years pass, if you don't rebalance, your portfolio will get unruly. Target date funds purport to do all that messy managing for you, but I find that many people aren't happy with their lack of flexibility. Also, as you progress in your career, you'll probably move to different employers and will want to roll your 401(k) savings over to an IRA or Roth IRA, in which you can manage the money yourself or have a professional do it for you. It's critical that you do this the right way or you can lose many of your hard-saved dollars to the tax man. Most important: do not touch the money yourself. The best way to accomplish this is to find a broker, financial adviser, or fund company to set up an IRA that can receive savings from your 401(k). Next, call the company's human resources department and get the form to do a direct rollover. Follow the directions to the letter. Your adviser or the fund company will assist. Remember, they are eager to have your dollars under their umbrella. Transfer the funds electronically to your IRA account or send a check payable to the new custodian (not you), which you can then deposit in your IRA account. For me, managing my retirement dollars over time is critical. Small details matter. For example, waiting until the eleventh hour to make an annual contribution to your IRA can cost you money. Many people wait until tax time to fund an IRA so that they can get the tax advantage. But losing those precious months during which your money could have been growing is a mistake that could cost you thousands of dollars over time.

WHEN TO HIRE A FINANCIAL ADVISER

In your twenties or even your thirties you may not need an adviser. Presumably, you'll be in wealth accumulation mode, and frankly, there just won't be that much to manage. Your biggest challenge will be to set up a solid 401(k), picking the right assortment of mutual funds to grow your money over time. Truth is, you don't need a human being to make this happen. Sophisticated software tools are available to average consumers through so-called robo-advisers; these are websites such as Betterment and Wealthfront. Costs are low. However, once your life gets more complicated—you have children, buy a home, or start your own business—a smart financial adviser can save you a lot of headaches. Good advisers don't just recommend investments for your 401(k); they help set up college savings plans and estate plans and assist with tax planning. I use an adviser and am glad I do. It's hard for regular investors to keep their attention focused on the long haul, but an adviser can do that for you. Anyone can put out a shingle and call himself or herself a financial planner, but you'll want to choose someone who has the best training. A CFP (Certified Financial Planner) designation is a good one and requires that the holder have at least three years of education in 100 different financial planning topics from estate planning to asset protection. Designees have to pass a rigorous exam to qualify. Choosing an adviser who is fee-only rather than paid by commission is the best course, because your adviser is more likely to be attuned to your bottom line rather than the latest product they want to sell. I know some folks who feel that they have chosen the wrong adviser. That sentiment was particularly acute during the financial crisis of 2008–2009. But even in good times, problem advisers surface. The Financial Industry Regulatory Authority (FINRA) tracks adviser performance. Check anyone you're considering hiring or your existing adviser at www.brokercheck.finra.org to find out if he or she has been disciplined by regulators. Every year, FINRA logs thousands of complaints from consumers. In 2013, 6 percent of investors with assets less than $1 million switched financial advisers, and 85 percent of affluent investors reported being dissatisfied with their financial adviser in a recent survey. The bottom line is that you will need an adviser capable of explaining the investments he or she is promoting in a clear way and helping you understand the risks. If an adviser can't communicate without using complicated jargon, stay away. Your adviser must be accessible and listen to your concerns. He should provide a written road map that describes your goals and how you will get there. If you decide you're in a bad situation and want to get out, decide first who will manage your money next. Pulling the plug is as simple as writing an e-mail to your adviser telling her to stop buying or selling in your account and sending a copy to the firm's compliance officer and office manager. Your new adviser can assist in the rollover.

TAPPING YOUR INVESTMENTS (THE RIGHT WAY) IN RETIREMENT

The government has made tapping your retirement funds unbelievably tricky. In fact, some advisers believe that it is so complicated that many folks will fail, setting up the possibility that you could owe a huge tax bill if you miss the mark. Here are the basics of what you need to know. At age 70½, you must take what the government calls required minimum distributions in the next tax year from your retirement accounts, and by that I mean any account with tax-deferred contributions, such as IRAs and 401(k)s. Here's the issue: the rules for taking your very first RMD are different from the rules for succeeding years. Normally, annual withdrawals have to be made by December 31. But with that very first distribution, the IRS gives you extra time: you have, if you need it, until April 1 of the year after the calendar year in which you turn 70½ to take your first RMD. Is your head hurting? I don't blame you. And if you do it wrong and miss the deadline, the IRS will tax the amount that is not withdrawn at 50 percent! Understanding how much you have to take out of your accounts is even more difficult. The IRS maintains a calculator at its website (IRS.gov), but an adviser also can help you find the right number. If you have multiple IRAs, you should calculate the RMD for each account separately, although you can withdraw the total from a single IRA. That said, if you have different types of retirement plans, such as an IRA and a 401(k), RMDs must be taken separately from each kind of plan. My view is that the government has no business telling us how much we should take out of our retirement accounts each year. Whose business is it but our own?

Now that you know the government's point of view on how much to withdraw from your account, let's examine what most financial advisers say. After all, what really matters is not whether your savings outlast you but whether you outlast your savings. The rule of thumb used by most advisers is that you can withdraw 4 percent each year from your nest egg and that your money should last 30 years. Now, I have to say that many advisers are rethinking this number because inflation has been low for so long. Consider that the three-month Treasury bill was paying 0.03 percent recently—close to zero!—compared with 6 percent in the 1990s. The plummet in interest rates has been a massive strain on retirees. In other words, the old rules don't apply, and if the same low-interest-rate environment persists, we will all need to invest and save a lot more for retirement than we may have planned. The good news is that advisers are coming up with computer-generated plans to manage money in retirement to adjust withdrawal rates and investment allocations annually to take into consideration changes in the markets and a retiree's personal circumstances.

THE RETIREMENT OF THE FUTURE

There is no doubt in my mind that retirement is in flux. The idea that at age 65 we will all stop working and relax on the porch with an iced tea is over. We are experiencing a national deficit of enormous proportions when it comes to retirement savings. You probably already know that. But there is another threat to your retirement that you need to be vigilant about. It is my abiding fear that politicians in Washington will look to the retirement savings that Americans have and find a way to squeeze even more tax dollars from them. Our 401(k) plans, which hold $4.5 trillion, are taxed at the time we take our money out. Yet I worry that politicians won't be able to keep their hands off our savings. Already the Obama administration is looking for ways to shave some of our savings and reduce tax benefits for saving. This is a mistake, but be warned: there is an assault on 401(k) and IRA savings in Washington, and it is essential that we protect our investments for our future generations.

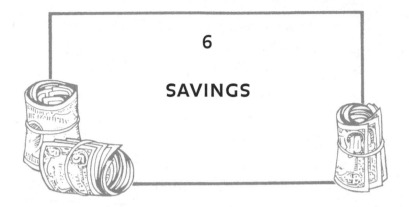

6

SAVINGS

When I was first discussing this book with potential publishing partners, one of them suggested writing a book about saving money. Wow, I thought; how quaint. *Nobody* talks about saving money. It seems so old-fashioned. Well, there is a reason for that: the Federal Reserve's policy of easy money (superlow interest rates) over the last seven years means there are virtually no rewards for saving money, certainly few that beat inflation. And even though it's better to build a nest egg than to spend money on things we don't need, it sure stings to get so small a return. The Obama administration also seems to have declared war on savers, targeting favored savings vehicles and attempting to limit their utility with higher taxes. In this chapter, we'll examine exactly how the government is making it more difficult to save and what you can do to fight back when you're attempting to put together a nest egg for a down payment for a home, college expenses, or retirement. I'll show you the best way to save and what to watch out for at every life stage. Remember, *saving is the first step in building wealth because without savings there is no investment.*

Ask any retiree. Saving money is difficult these days. Think about the placard in the neighborhood bank window. Is it advertising a 2 percent, 3 percent, or even 4 percent return on short-term money market funds? No, it's advertising a return barely more than 1 percent! At those levels, you're losing money to inflation. The Fed has kept rates near zero for seven years. There hasn't been a rate hike in a decade. Borrowers are thrilled (if they can get a loan), but savers of every age are devastated. Every day I report yet another study or survey showing how Americans are woefully undersaved for retirement. But what about the people who are already retired? How are they faring? The truth is that the Federal Reserve's policies are robbing their retirement caches. You simply can't make enough money to stay ahead of inflation by using conventional savings tools such as certificates of deposit and Treasuries.

How did we get to the point where the government could blithely redistribute wealth? Essentially, the government's policy during the Great Recession was to reward the profligate, those who couldn't pay their mortgages and banks that had gambled on complex mortgage investments. Remember? Here's the government response to the crisis in a nutshell.

On September 8, 2008, our Treasury seized control of Fannie Mae and Freddie Mac as the market for mortgage investments collapsed. A week later, the government bailed out the global insurer American International Group. Private lending by banks ground to a halt during this period, and the Fed responded by cutting interest rates. President George W. Bush signed into law a $700 billion bailout plan to assist the nation's lenders. After those first harried months of the crisis, the Fed embarked on a six-year program of stabilizing the nation's financial sector by buying trillions of dollars' worth of mortgage debt and Treasuries. In doing so, the Fed became a buyer of financial products and put a floor under government debt, dropping rates further. The Federal Reserve's method of effecting all this was simply to print money. Interest rates were held at zero for seven years. Follow-on programs by Presidents Bush and Obama extended forgiveness to mortgage borrowers who had made bad deals.

The impact of this unprecedented involvement of the Federal Reserve in the financial sector is that banks and borrowers who had made bad bets were bailed out while savers were hit with a one-two punch. First their stock investments cratered, with many losing 40 to 50 percent as the stock market went into free fall. Then, as they sought stability in savings vehicles, returns on conventional certificates of deposit, money market funds, and Treasuries collapsed. There was no place to run or hide for the most responsible among us. According to the reinsurer Swiss Re, the Fed's low- and no-rate policy cost savers $470 billion, an astonishing amount. Senior citizens suffer the most from low rates. According to a study from the Manhattan Institute, people 75 and older get 8 percent of their income from interest, dividends, and rents. Think of it this way: if you invested your retirement in one-month Treasuries under this Fed, it would take nearly 1,400 years to double your money. And that's not the only effect low rates are having on the elderly. Low rates are causing premiums on long-term care insurance policies to skyrocket, and annuity payouts are falling to all-time lows. There are impacts for younger savers too. Putting together a down payment for a home becomes infinitely harder if the earnings on your savings are low. College savers are penalized similarly. In short, the Fed's policy of low rates has been a boon for lenders and the markets but not for the rest of us.

Bashing the Fed is seen as the preserve of the far right. Libertarians demand an end to the Federal Reserve or ask for audits of the system. But voices of discontent can be found across the political spectrum. The Left thinks the Fed is too close to Wall Street, whereas mainstream Republicans worry that easy money has fueled a stock market boom that is unsustainable. Most mainstream financial journalists simply shrug when they hear these criticisms, but it's time to think seriously about the enormous power the Federal Reserve has accumulated. The entire federal government is built on the idea of checks and balances that are intended to limit power. The House and Senate can make laws, but the president has to sign them. The Supreme Court can, in the end, override both the president and Congress. The idea is that no one branch of government can monopolize power. But the opposite is true of the Federal Reserve. Neither the members of the Board of Governors nor the chair is elected. Instead, the president appoints each with approval from the Senate. Board members serve 14 years (an eternity in Washington), but Fed chairs can serve for even longer. Alan Greenspan held the leadership post of the largest central bank in the free world for 19 years, having been appointed by Ronald Reagan in 1987 and serving three more presidents before his retirement in 2006.

With that power has come major criticism. Greenspan's easy money policies, which is to say his penchant for keeping interest rates low, are all too well known and helped cause the dot-com boom and subsequent bust. It's no surprise that a housing boom and bust followed. What is shocking to me is that there was never a serious reevaluation of the policies that ultimately played a role in the housing and financial crisis that plunged the economy into recession beginning in December 2007. Greenspan's replacement, Ben Bernanke, kept rates near zero throughout the recession, and his successor, Janet Yellen, has done the same thing even as the economy has developed increasing momentum and strength. Many wonder whether the Fed is setting us up again for another bubble that bursts, creating yet another crisis that it will have to manage by—you guessed it—lowering rates.

Ironically, it was a financial crisis that led Congress to set up the Fed in the first place. The Panic of 1907 in which the stock market quickly lost 50 percent of its value and a resulting wave of fear led to a run on banks, was the seed that led to the Fed's founding with the passage of the Federal Reserve Act in 1913. When Lawrence White, a George Mason University economist, assessed the performance of the Fed on the hundredth anniversary of its founding, he concluded that the institution had presided over more rather than fewer periods of monetary and economic instability, which was the reason for setting up the Fed in the first place.

It's not just the Fed that is crippling savers' efforts. The White House has shown little interest in supporting individual savers. Some of the most prized savings vehicles for Americans, such as 529 plans for college savers and 401(k) retirement savings plans, have been attacked by the Obama administration. In his 2015 State of the Union address, the president announced his intention of eliminating the tax benefits of 529 plans, the savings accounts parents use to set aside money for their children's college education tax-free. (Read on to find out how best to take advantage of 529s.) In its place, the president proposed a government-sponsored program to enroll college-age students in community colleges for two years. Neither suggestion received broad support. Similarly, his idea of capping retirement savings in tax-sheltered retirement accounts drew fire from retirement experts who said the limits would affect 1 in 10 savers negatively.

These pressures make it more difficult than ever to manage your savings effectively. What can you do to protect yourself from the policies of the Fed and the president and set aside money for your important life goals? Read on. I've organized this chapter with an eye to the life cycle of saving. I start with those newly on their own and just getting started and work my way through saving for a home, college, and finally retirement.

GETTING STARTED

First things first. To my mind, half of being successful financially boils down to avoiding fees or charges you shouldn't be paying and squeezing a little extra something out of every penny you have. That rule goes double in a low-interest-rate environment because you can't use high yields to cover your mistakes. It's important to get started on the right foot. Think of saving money as something you will always be doing because once you achieve one goal, such as paying off college debt or assembling a down payment for a house, there will be a new goal. Because you'll be saving over decades, every monthly charge matters. Start by choosing a bank that is interested in having you as a client.

That means you want to open an account at an institution that doesn't charge a monthly fee for the privilege of holding your money in a checking account. Fully 38 percent of checking accounts have no fee, and many banks will waive the fee if you agree to have your paycheck deposited in that account, maintain a preset balance, or use e-statements. Interest-bearing accounts generally aren't worth the effort these days because of the low returns they offer and the high balances they require. Average interest-bearing account balance requirements rose in 2014 to $6,211, and the fee if you don't meet those requirements rose as well. Yields, according to Bankrate.com, were just 0.04 percent, pretty punk, and if your balance dips below the balance requirements—well, did I mention that I don't like fees? However, I am a fan of the old-fashioned bank because deposits up to $250,000 are guaranteed by the federal government. You might think that doesn't matter, but we tested those limits in 2008, remember? Banks, even some of the biggest, were perilously close to shuttering. So go with a bank. Prepaid debit cards are a poor alternative because of their lack of backstops and their exorbitant fees. What's more, you can't buy a certificate of deposit from Justin Bieber's prepaid debit card issuer, right? It's a one-trick pony not worthy of your attention. I like solid midsize regional banks and credit unions because they can make local decisions to accommodate serious savers like yourself.

Once you get your account set up, you'll want to begin

saving. Think of paying yourself first when it comes to saving. In the best-case scenario, you'll be setting aside 12 to 15 percent of your gross income for the future. The best way to do this is to set aside this money before you can get your hands on it. You'll never miss what you never had access to. Set up a separate account with an automatic deposit from your main checking account. This will be your emergency savings fund. Keep it at the bank, where it can be accessed immediately. Ultimately you'll want six months' worth of living expenses set aside for the inevitable car repair or dental bill that comes along. You can contribute to that emergency fund over time and, once you hit your goal, start saving for something else.

SETTING UP YOUR 401(K)

If you're working, set up a 401(k) at the office. If you can afford to, set aside the maximum of $18,000 each year. If you can't manage that, put aside as much as you can—ideally up to the level that your employer matches. People age 50 and over can set aside an additional $6,000 each year. This may sound like a lot, but remember that inflation even at its current low, low levels will cut the value of your savings over long periods. These days corporate 401(k)s tend to offer shorter menus of options. You're safest starting out with index funds and exchange-traded funds with superlow fees (this was covered in Chapter 5). The matching contribution from your employer can often be 50 cents to a dollar for every dollar you contribute, up to a set maximum of 3 to 6 percent of your salary. This is free money that you shouldn't hesitate to get. Young investors should remember that the employer's match typically vests over time. That means that if you leave the company before the vesting period ends, usually three to four years, you will not walk away with that money. Otherwise, the matching funds are yours to keep.

SAVING FOR A HOME

One of the first big purchases you're likely to make is a home. Putting together a down payment can be tough. The trick is to make it automatic. Start by finding out whether you can afford to buy a home by calculating the difference between your current housing costs and your projected monthly mortgage payment for an entry-level home or co-op and save that additional amount each month. This will help you get a feel for the impact a housing payment will have on your monthly budget without taking on the risk of actually having one. By test-driving the impact of a housing payment on your monthly budget, you'll be less likely to spend too much on a home when you do purchase one. Just remember that lenders will not want your housing payments to be more than 28 percent of your gross monthly pay, and a mortgage shouldn't bring total debt to more than 36 percent of your gross monthly pay. Down payments for first-time buyers can be as much as 3 percent to 20 percent of the purchase price of a home. Find out the average price for an entry-level home in your area and create a monthly savings plan for reaching your goal. It's important to set a deadline so that other expenses don't get in the way. A word to the anxious: your goal may seem difficult to achieve, but patience is important here. Once you achieve your goal, you'll continue to set aside savings for new goals. Getting in the habit of saving is critical because once you buy the house, you'll have other financial goals.

SAVING FOR COLLEGE

Far and away the best vehicle for parents (and grandparents) to save for college is the 529 savings plan. The tax advantages are simply unrivaled. You set aside money for your children's education, and you tap it tax-free. Some states even offer deductions to parents who contribute to the state 529. The ceiling on the amounts that can be set aside in these accounts (more than $300,000 in most states) is so high as to be nonexistent for most savers. No other savings account gets such favorable treatment. We can thank former

President George W. Bush for that. The college savings plans were introduced in 2001 as part of his tax cuts.

The plans come in a couple of different flavors. There are savings plans that work like a 401(k) or IRA, which means you contribute monthly to an account invested in mutual funds that you choose from a list. Your account rises and falls with the market. Prepaid plans allow you to pay all or part of in-state public college fees up front. It may be converted for use at other institutions as well. Prepaid plans may be priced above today's tuition rates. Check to be sure. Nearly every state has a 529 option, and now that you can use the proceeds of virtually any savings plan in any state, you should pick the state with the best track record when you are ready to invest. One reliable website for checking the performance of 529 plans is SavingForCollege.com. Not only can you find the top 10 performers, you can dig into other details about saving for college. At the time of this writing, Tennessee, New York, and Michigan had the best one-year plan returns. And remember, you can always invest in more than one state's plan after you've maxed those benefits. As you shop, compare fees. More than half of 529 investors buy broker-sold plans, which carry sales charges and offer more investment options. If you don't want to pay the fees for advice, pick a plan that offers a solid handful of low-cost index funds from a company such as Vanguard or Fidelity.

SAVING FOR RETIREMENT

People spend an inordinate amount of time thinking about how much to save for retirement, sometimes to the exclusion of actually setting aside money. Many of us, myself included, become obsessed with figuring out "the right number" because in our minds having a hard and fast goal makes it easier to plan. But the other reason, and I think the real reason, we are so keen on finding that number is that we believe that it represents safety. Once we hit that goal, ah! We're safe. Retirement will be a breeze. Unfortunately, that's not quite true. Situations change. Personal finance is really interpersonal. Your spouse or partner may find that the pension he or she was relying on isn't available. Or maybe a relative leaves you a considerable bequest. Don't get me wrong; I'm not saying you shouldn't plan. But I am saying that flexibility is key. The reality is that different people will need very different amounts in retirement depending on their circumstances and expectations.

Even the experts disagree about the best way to calculate the number. Your financial adviser may ask you how much of your current income you'll want to spend in retirement. This is tricky because you probably have little idea of your likely spending patterns once your career is in the rearview mirror. What's more, your spending may be far different in early retirement from what it is later. Others believe that the best way to plan is to hit a savings goal that is a multiple of your ending salary, which presumably will be the highest you are ever paid. Fidelity, for example, has advocated saving eight times your ending salary, assuming you're financing 25 years of retirement. The folks at Fidelity believe you should work up to this level of savings, putting away one times your current salary at age 35, three times your current salary by 45, and five times your current salary by 55. By following this formula, Fidelity estimates, retirees will be able to replace 85 percent of their final annual salaries. Benefits consultants at Aon Hewitt believe Fidelity is onto something but recommend a higher multiple of 11 times one's ending salary. The mutual fund company T. Rowe Price has recommended 12 times one's ending salary. Here's another way to think about it from a company called BTN Research: for every $1,000 of monthly income you want in retirement, you need $269,000 in the bank at retirement. For example, an individual who wants $60,000 a year in retirement, or $5,000 a month (in addition to any pensions and Social Security), would need to have saved $1.35 million by the time he or she retired. Of course, all these rules of thumb have hidden assumptions about annual investment returns and consistency of saving that may prove inaccurate in the real world.

Here's a simpler way to think about retirement savings. You probably know that whatever your final number is, experts recommend spending no more than 4 percent of that total every year. That's the rate of withdrawal that is most likely to stretch your savings over a long enough period to last your lifetime. Let's work backward from there. If you believe you'll need $100,000 to live on each year (after Social Security), your number should be $2.5 million. That's $100,000 divided by 0.04. This is, admittedly, a back-of-the-envelope calculation. To figure out how close you are to this target, start by multiplying your current savings by 0.04 percent. This will tell you how much you could withdraw each year from your current savings. If you have $850,000 saved, you could pull out $34,000 a year. Add in an annual value of your home equity by dividing your total home equity by the number of years you expect to live. If you are 55 and expect to live to 95 and have $300,000 in home equity, the annual value of your real estate is $7,500 a year. Add in any inheritance, again divided by the number of years you expect to live. Add in annual pension benefits, Social Security benefits, and any other remaining income you expect to get.

Fortunately, there are many calculators on the Web that can help you determine what your number should be. If you are between 55 and 64, BlackRock Investments uses current data—interest rates, inflation, and others—to calculate a potential annual income given your current savings. The Vanguard Retirement Income Calculator packs huge computing capability into its calculator, which delivers potential monthly retirement income that is based on a range of investment returns that you choose and allows you to add in Social Security and pension incomes. Sliders allow you to finesse the data. Finally, the MarketWatch Retirement Plan allows you to add in factors such as home equity and taxable accounts. I like the way it helps you visualize your income in retirement.

One word of warning: a lot can happen over 25 or 30 years of retirement. You can expect inflation over three decades of retirement to cut your spending power in half. Medical costs are escalating, and estimates of the cost of hospital and doctor bills not covered by Medicare range from $230,000 to $450,000. Carrying debt into retirement changes all the estimates of how long your savings will last. According to the New York Federal Reserve, Americans age 60 and over owe $36 billion of student debt. The most useful rule of thumb for most savers who aren't yet at the threshold of retirement is to try to save 15 percent of your gross income for retirement over your working life. That should provide a nest egg that can provide you with 85 percent of your final year's salary. Remember that you're likely to live a long time. Experts predict that today's 65-year-old has a 45 percent chance of reaching 90. Plan for living for a long time.

SAVING MONEY IN RETIREMENT

No doubt retirees are in the tightest spot when it comes to navigating a low-rate environment because their prime earning years are behind them. They can't go out and make up for the fact that their money is earning precious little in conventional savings vehicles such as money market funds, certificates of deposit, and savings accounts. Every year their dollars lose buying power to inflation. One analysis of those trends showed that bank account depositors lost $635 billion in buying power in the four years that followed the end of the recession as inflation ate into their savings. It's no wonder that retirees are facing major headwinds. A Kaiser Family Foundation analysis of Census Bureau poverty estimates for seniors found that 9 percent of people 65 and older live in poverty. Add in other information such as out-of-pocket medical costs and the high cost of housing, and 15 percent of seniors are living in poverty.

The answer for many seniors will be shopping around for the best returns and not locking down too much money in 5- or 10-year certificates of deposit in case interest rates zoom higher. Currently, the spread on rates paid on products such as certificates of deposit aren't very wide. Yes, some of the most competitive will pay 5-year rates that are double the rates on 1-year CDs, but the difference is still only a single percentage point at this writing. When rates are so low and the difference between those on short-term investments and those on longer-term ones is so small, it makes sense to keep your powder dry. Sure, use CDs, but don't lock up your money in long-terms CDs so that you can take advantage of rate hikes when they do finally occur. Websites such as Bankrate.com can help you figure out which institutions in your area are offering the best rates. One piece of advice here: the most generous terms typically are offered by online banks because they are trying to grow their business. Finally, don't get too carried away with investing in stocks. You still need to keep some of your money in cash. In the last few years, stocks have been on a roll, but that can change quickly. It's important to invest in stocks, which historically—over time—do deliver better returns than does parking your money in a bank account. But decide what proportion you want to keep in the market and stay on top of that asset allocation.

When it comes to the markets, you'll want to look for investments that offer income. Dividend-paying stocks are a good place to start. Fortunately, you'll find plenty of mutual fund offerings, both traditional and ETFs, that can fill the bill without your being forced to double down on a single company. Other options that deliver income include high-quality bonds and real estate investment trusts.

Next, let's look at some of the products you may be tempted to turn to in a low-rate environment, such as rising-rate certificates of deposit. According to Bankrate.com, which surveyed 150 banks and credit unions, these products almost always favor the financial institution. They include the following:

Liquid or no-penalty CDs: These products promise private investors a way to access some or all of their investment before maturity without a penalty. However, Bankrate found that three- and five-year liquid CDs with yields higher than 1.05 percent still fell short of what could be obtained on top-yielding, nationally available three- and five-year traditional CDs.

BUMP-UP CDs: These products give investors the option to increase their rate at some point during the term the product is held if interest rates rise. However, the yields offered on bump-up CDs covered in the survey fell short of those of the top-yielding national traditional CDs of the same maturity, often by a wide margin. According to Bankrate, there is simply no hope of bumping up enough to offset the lower initial yield. The highest-yielding two-year bump-up CD in the survey paid 0.85 percent, whereas the top-yielding national available traditional two-year CD paid 1.5 percent.

STEP-UP CDs: These products promise predetermined increases in the rate at specified periods during the term. In all the cases analyzed by Bankrate, the blended interest rate fell short of that of the top-yielding traditional CD.

CALLABLE CDs: These products can be called in before maturity at the issuing financial institution's discretion. If the yield is attractive, they probably will be called so that the institutions can reissue at a lower yield. The result? A heads you win, tails you lose proposition.

In short, these new innovations on certificates of deposit are no replacement for the old-fashioned original.

MANAGING THE BIG KAHUNA: SOCIAL SECURITY

In such a low-rate environment, it's more critical than ever that you manage your Social Security as carefully as possible. In Chapter 1, I wrote extensively about the spiraling costs of entitlement programs and criticized the increasing number of Americans who rely on the government to pay their freight through antipoverty programs such as SNAP and unemployment benefits. But Social Security, as Fox Business Network viewers continually remind me, is different. If you've worked throughout your life, you've paid into Social Security's "lock box," as Al Gore used to call it. That's the line item on your paycheck called FICA, or the Federal Insurance Contributions Act. In other words, it's *your money.* You salted away Social Security savings each and every year, and it's only right that as you retire, you take what you are due. Here's how it works: once *you* qualify for benefits, so may your spouse, your ex-spouse, your younger children, your disabled children, and even your parents. These folks could receive benefits on the basis of your work record. The flip side is true as well. You can receive spousal benefits, survivor benefits, and divorcee survivor benefits that are based on the work records of current or even former spouses.

What's astonishing to me is just how much money Social Security represents for so many families—*over time.* Imagine a 60-year-old couple that starts working at age 25, paying $22,900 in 1979 in FICA, the maximum at that time. Over the years, they continue to work and continue to contribute the maximum amounts to Social Security. (The maximum income level at which Social Security tax was assessed was $118,500 in 2015.) If they retired at age 66 and began collecting benefits, they'd get $31,972 per year each, or $63,944 together. That stream of payments from Social Security would be worth $1.2 million over time, according to Boston University professor Laurence Kotlikoff's excellent book *Get What's Yours* (he also sells a $40 online tool at Maximize MySocialSecurity.com). Most people don't have that much money saved even when they include the value of their home. As Kotlikoff told me, Social Security for most people will be their biggest asset or one of their biggest assets when they retire. Therefore, deciding to take those benefits can make a huge difference in how much you collect over your lifetime. Being patient and waiting to take the benefits can have a huge consequence. Consider our couple who retired at age 66 after a lifetime of maximum FICA contributions. If they had waited until age 70 to take Social Security benefits, delaying just four years after what Social Security calls their full retirement age, they would have collected $42,203 individually per year, or $84,406 together—fully a third more. According to Kotlikoff, that represents lifetime collections of $1.6 million. A good rule of thumb is that taking retirement benefits at age 70 will result in lifetime benefits 76 percent higher than that of people who start taking benefits at the earliest age possible, 62.

But the devil here is in the details. Despite the fact that most retirees rely on Social Security for 50 percent or more of their retirement income, a lot of us are leaving money on the table. As I mentioned, waiting to take benefits is important, but it's also necessary to understand all the benefits you may be eligible for. The list includes the following: retirement insurance benefit, spouse's insurance benefits, divorced spouse's insurance benefits, child-in-care spouse's insurance benefits, widow(er) insurance benefits, child insurance benefits, disabled child insurance benefits, and surviving child insurance benefits. But here is the Social Security Administration's big gotcha: you can't take two benefits at the same time. Instead, the SSA will pay you the larger of the two, and if you file for *your* retirement benefits, it will wipe out any spousal or divorced spousal benefit if you try to take both benefits at the same time. The trick, says Kotlikoff, is to optimize benefits, ensuring that you get the *greater* of the benefits you are eligible for. According to the Center for Retirement Research, most Americans don't do that, leaving as much as $10 billion on the table *each year.* Plus, there are traps in Social Security that can reduce your benefits forever.

For example, according to Kotlikoff, if you get divorced from your spouse just one day shy of 10 years of marriage, neither you nor your spouse will collect a dime in spousal benefits.

TAPPING YOUR RETIREMENT SAVINGS

I have to think that few things are more nerve-wracking than breaking into your retirement nest egg for the first time. After all, you've spent your entire working life making sure to leave your retirement savings alone (at least I hope you haven't tapped your savings). When you decide to retire and start taking money out, you'll want to make sure you meet the federal requirements so that you don't owe a huge tax bill. The rules are the following: You must take your required minimum withdrawal (RMD) by April 1 of the year after you turn 70½. This applies to tax-deferred accounts such as IRAs, 401(k)s, 403(b)s, and 457(b)s but not to Roth IRAs, in which taxes are paid up front. Normally, annual withdrawals must be made by December 31, but the IRS gives you a little more time with the first withdrawal. The amount of the RMD is based on a uniform life expectancy table in IRS Publication 590 and the amount in your plan. The RMD is calculated by dividing the year-end account value by the life expectancy value. If you run afoul of these rules and fail to take an RMD, you owe taxes of *50 percent* on the amount that is not withdrawn! Amazingly, 59 percent of Fidelity

Investment customers had not taken the full RMDs from their IRAs as of December 26, 2014, and 43 percent hadn't taken any money out at all. Frankly, I think the entire idea of a required minimum distribution is ridiculous—and the penalties, of course, are even worse. To my mind, you saved your retirement nest egg and should be allowed to access it any way you want. Obviously, federal tax law doesn't agree with that view and applies a heavy penalty to people who ignore the rules. It's cold comfort that you can turn around and invest that money in a brokerage account if you like.

In subsequent years, you'll want to minimize the tax bite. Leave your money in tax-deferred accounts such as an IRA or 401(k) as long as you can to allow that balance to continue to grow without the drag of taxes. In the early years, take some of your money from taxable accounts as well as tax-deferred accounts so that you pay the lowest possible tax rates on withdrawals. By keeping withdrawals at a level of 4 percent of your total savings you'll give yourself the best chance of not outliving your money. If you can't get by on a 4 percent withdrawal rate, you may want to consider downsizing or taking out a reverse mortgage to make up the difference. If you're able to follow my advice and wait until age 70 to take Social Security but still want to retire at 65, there are a couple of ways to draw income from your savings. You can take cash out of your savings or convert some of those savings into an annuity. For every $10,000 you have in savings (in an account managed for income, not growth), you can draw

$400 a year, or $33 a month, and not affect your balance, according to the Financial Security Project at Boston College. In other words, if you have $1 million in retirement savings, you can withdraw $40,000 a year to pay the bills and not worry that your money will evaporate. Another option would be to buy an annuity that pays $500 a year, or $42 a month, for every $10,000 you invest. Most retirees can come up with an estimate of their monthly costs, but determining medical costs over time is nearly impossible. Medicare will pay many of your healthcare costs in retirement, but you will be responsible for premiums, co-pays, deductibles, and other items that Medicare doesn't cover. Private Medigap policies can make up much of the difference. However, the big exception is long-term care. Although Medicaid pays for nursing home care for people with low income and few assets, others have to fund the cost themselves. Considering that one-quarter of Americans over age 65 are expected to spend an average of one year in a nursing home at a cost of $75,000, it makes sense to consider buying a long-term-care insurance policy. The cost is about $200 a month for a policy bought at age 65 that pays up to $60,000 a year.

MY LAST SAVINGS WORD

The single biggest mistake I see American families making when it comes to saving is spending too much money on their kids. I understand the impulse. All parents want to give their children the best of everything. This becomes particularly troublesome during the college years, when parents know all too well how difficult it is to start one's adult life with a heavy debt burden. But the sad truth is this: no one is going to pay for your retirement but you. There are loans for college but not for retirement. Prioritize your savings just as you do paying off debt. Your retirement should be a top priority.

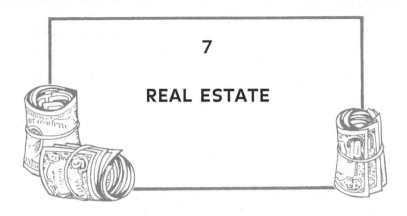

7

REAL ESTATE

I want to start this chapter on home ownership by putting my cards on the table. I've been a longtime advocate of home ownership as a way to build overall wealth. In my book *Home Rich*, I argued that any single expense that commands a third of my income month in and month out—as a mortgage does—better give me a decent return for my trouble. Makes sense, right? You set aside money over time, and you get paid back and then some. To be completely up front, I am one of the people who got caught in the housing bubble. No, I wasn't foreclosed on and my husband and I never owed more than our house was worth, but if we had been forced to sell our home in the depths of the housing market crash, we would have lost money. A lot of it. Our home's value fell like a stone, as did that of other properties in our neighborhood. It was a nail-biting two years or so that I never want to revisit.

Like a lot of Americans, I had done nothing to deserve this kind of rough treatment. My husband and I had chosen the property, a 1933 Tudor in the New York City suburbs, carefully, making sure we didn't overextend ourselves. We put down 20 percent on the purchase price to get a good start. In short, we did everything right. But as we were making those choices, the stars were aligning for trouble. Ill-considered Washington policies encouraging home ownership that had been in place for decades finally came home to roost. If you're trying to build your wealth, it's critical that you understand how all this came to pass and ended up robbing average, everyday Americans of $6.6 trillion in home values, a mind-blowing 30 percent of the market. In this chapter I'll reveal the roots of the housing debacle and share the critical lessons for buyers, sellers, and home owners. As the market continues to struggle with the legacy of the downturn, I'll show you how to manage your most important asset as a home owner: your equity.

ROOT CAUSES

Let's start by reviewing the causes of the worst housing sell-off in American history. It's conventional wisdom that Wall Street banks were at the center of the trouble, but although those institutions did play an important role, they didn't set in motion the events that resulted in the free fall in home prices. Government, in my opinion, knocked over the first domino that set the debacle in motion. In Chapter 1, I described how the federal government's policy of expanding home ownership, especially among lower-income households, had become a bipartisan national goal. In recent years, every president from Bill Clinton to Barack Obama has eagerly pursued such policies. Republicans, too, have been on board. President George W. Bush backed the idea, saying, "If you own something, you have a vital stake in the future of the country." Enforcing such a massive social policy requires more than just a little dabbling in the markets, and Congress found the tools it needed for the job in two quasi-governmental entities: Fannie Mae and Freddie Mac. Chartered way back in 1938, Fannie Mae was designed simply to purchase home mortgages from banks and savings and loans so that those lenders could in effect recycle the money to underwrite additional housing loans. Freddie Mac came along in 1970 to do pretty much the same thing.

Not long afterward, the mortgage-backed security was invented, a pass-through certificate, as it was called back then. The idea was simple and effective: instead of selling entire mortgages to investors created by the system, why not pool mortgages and allow investors to buy pieces of the pie? For investors, the attractions were two: ease of use and a reduction in default risk, since a lot of mortgages were pooled, lessening the effect of any one mortgage defaulting. As it turned out, securitizing mortgages—turning mortgage loans into tradable investments—was like giving crack cocaine to Wall Street. The mortgage securities market grew like Topsy. At its peak in 2011, the market for mortgage-related securities topped $8 trillion. The beauty of this from Congress's point of view was that the government could fulfill its federally mandated housing goals without having to spend a dime. All it had to do was require Freddie Mac and Fannie Mae to buy a set proportion of mortgages sold to lower-income borrowers. Initially, government policy required that 30 percent of the mortgages purchased by Freddie and Fannie be made to low- and middle-income borrowers. During the Clinton administration that requirement was raised to 50 percent. Bush raised the goal to an astonishing 56 percent. In other words, the *government* was the marketplace for the majority of Americans seeking home ownership.

Everybody seemed to benefiting, at least at first. Home-buyers were happy because of the increased access to capital and the low down payment requirements. Banks were making a mint. But as the housing boom wore on, it became more and more difficult to fill the government quota without lending to people who were only marginally qualified to get a mortgage or, worse, not qualified at all. Securitizations expanded beyond the traditional prime loans to include sub-prime and Alt-A loans: loans to people with subpar credit and an unpredictable income. The proportion of borrowers who paid 3 percent of the purchase price as a down payment jumped from 1 in 230 in 1989 to 1 in 3 in 2007. As a sign of just how crazy and overextended the market had become, lenders started issuing NINJA loans, which means loans to individuals or couples with no income and no assets. A borrower didn't need verifiable income anymore to get a mortgage, just a wink and a promise. Due diligence became a thing of the past.

Countrywide's CEO, Angelo Mozilo, reportedly told his employees that he could tell whether a borrower would repay a loan by looking him or her in the eye. Mozilo, a consummate salesman, came to symbolize much of what was wrong with the market. The perma-tanned flashy dresser's lending operation practiced some of the most liberal lending practices in the industry, underwriting an astonishing $490 billion in mortgages in 2006. From the bankers' point of view that was good. It meant that there was a bevy of choices on the mortgage investment store shelf for investors with every risk profile, from conventional mortgages with hefty down payments to ones that were more of a crap shoot. Even Fannie and Freddie got in on the action by investing *directly* in mortgages, amassing portfolios of mortgage securities worth $1.5 trillion. Yesterday's sober government agency had become in essence a hedge fund operating on the government's dime and eating its own product.

As a result, home prices skyrocketed, and the housing bubble expanded even as the unintended consequences of the government's misguided policies were beginning to bear fruit. Affordable housing requirements, ironically, reduced the very affordability they sought to increase. The lower the down payment requirement becomes, the bigger and more expensive houses buyers can afford. At 10 percent down, a buyer with $10,000 can afford a $100,000 home by using that $10,000 as a down payment. But drop the down payment requirement to 5 percent and the same buyer can upgrade to a $200,000 house. Therefore, prices rise and affordability wanes. Not only were the government quotas a major contributor to the housing crash—lax loans defaulted at a steep rate—they also failed in their goal of raising home ownership levels, which have fluctuated between 62 and 65 percent in recent years. Before these policies were enacted, home ownership rates were 63.9 percent.

On the backs of these shoddy lending standards that government policy actively endorsed, the market for mortgage-related securities grew to $8.5 trillion by 2011. And then it all came crashing down. By the time the housing market was in free fall in 2007, every week seemed to bring news of a subprime lender failure or the implosion of another bank's mortgage portfolio. I was covering the debacle and watched it gather steam. In January of that year, the legendary Wall Street investment bank Bear Stearns liquidated two funds invested in subprime mortgages. A month later, Freddie Mac announced it no longer would buy subprime loans. Credit grew scarce as banks became hesitant to lend. By December 2007, the economy was in recession. A month later, Angelo

Mozilo was forced to sell Countrywide to Bank of America. The choice was dire: sell or go bankrupt.

September 2008 marked the nadir of the crisis, with every day bringing fresh and disturbing headlines. By that point, the credit crisis was in full swing as lenders stopped lending. The value of mortgage investments plummeted, and with it the stability of Fannie Mae and Freddie Mac, which experienced losses of nearly $15 billion. Henry Paulson, the U.S. Treasury secretary, announced that the government would place the two entities in "conservatorship," formalizing an assumed government backing with $200 billion in taxpayer money. The move was unprecedented and put the government in uncharted waters. Rumors filled the newsrooms. Speculation became the house game. What if you went to an ATM and couldn't get money out? What if all the major banks failed? Truth is, we came close to just that. On the heels of the government bailout of Fannie and Freddie, American International Group, the world's biggest insurer, was bailed out with taxpayer money. Lehman Brothers, a venerable Wall Street player in the bond market, imploded and filed for bankruptcy. Federal regulators closed Washington Mutual Bank, which became the biggest bank failure in history. On October 3, 2008, Bush signed into law TARP, the Troubled Asset Relief Program, a $700 billion bailout of Wall Street.

Seven years later, we're still struggling with the legacy of the housing crash and the resulting implosion of the financial sector. The economy continues to struggle. Although the recovery began six years ago, the U.S. economy hasn't produced a single year of growth above 3 percent since 2009. Worse, the federal government has plunged even deeper into the housing markets. Fannie Mae and Freddie Mac guaranteed 27 percent of all mortgages in 2006. By 2012, that proportion stood at 69 percent. Retribution seeking by state attorneys general and the federal government reached record highs. Fines against banks for their roles in the crisis have totaled $100 billion. The biggest levies fell on the biggest banks: JPMorgan Chase, Bank of America, Citigroup, and Wells Fargo. Yet bewilderingly, President Obama has continued to try to increase home ownership rates. More bizarre, tighter regulations enacted because of the housing crash were abandoned at the administration's direction. Regulators had required a down payment of 20 percent and maximum debt-to-income ratios of 36 percent. Under Obama's watch, down payment requirements have returned to 3 percent and debt-to-income limits have risen to 43 percent. Mel Watt, a North Carolina legislator whom Obama appointed to run the government's housing policy, is a longtime advocate of affordable housing who continues to push the very affordable housing goals that got us in trouble in the first place. He's delayed congressional requirements that Fannie Mae and Freddie Mac increase the fees they charge to guarantee loans. That just might get the mortgage market standing on its own two feet and discourage government participation, but Watt wants to keep things the way they are and advocates what is really a creeping nationalization of housing that inevitably will lead to the same problems we had in the recent past.

The crash in housing prices has convinced many people that home ownership is a bad deal. It's almost impossible, for example, to read the business pages in the newspaper and not see a story about how younger potential buyers have decided that ownership is not for them. Millennials are happy enough, so the stories go, with their smartphones and a set of Beats wireless headphones. I can hardly blame anyone for losing faith. After all, the plummet in prices and the seizing up in the market are unparalleled in our lifetimes. With the exception of the savings and loan crisis in the late 1980s and early 1990s, home prices had been on an upward trajectory year in and year out since 1963. That kind of consistency is without parallel in the stock and bond markets, which are far more cyclical. For that reason, few could see the crash coming. I remember arguing with the economist for the National Association of Realtors about whether prices could fall at the height of the boom at a convention for housing industry players. No, he said. There could be regional price breaks, single markets where prices could crater, but no national spiral downward. As we debated, Realtors who had benefited from the bubble chattered happily around us. What could go wrong? The market was on fire! But it was all about to change dramatically. After housing prices in

Arizona, California, Florida, and Nevada recorded gains of more than 25 percent in 2005 over 2004, prices nationally edged down 3.3 percent in the first quarter of 2006 from the previous quarter. And that was just the start. I can hardly blame that economist for not seeing the 30 percent gap down in prices that was coming, but it would have been nice if someone had warned consumers about the disaster on the horizon.

I believe that over those years before and even after the crash we got into the habit of analyzing our personal housing wealth by following housing prices to the exclusion of anything else. Price appreciation, we'd come to believe, was the name of the game. I disagree. Price gains are only part of the story. I know we talk about home ownership and home owners, but the reality is this: unless you've paid off your mortgage loan, your lender owns your house. What home owners actually own is their *equity,* which in its simplest and most frequently used definition is the value of their payments (including the down payment) minus monthly interest costs. Truth is, price appreciation is just one part of your return when you sell a house. The other part, and the thing many people have ignored, is their contribution in the form of mortgage payments and renovations. Equity includes all of this plus appreciation. The good news is that you pay your mortgage each and every month no matter whether housing prices are going up or down. There is no equivalent for renters. Renters send off their monthly check, and that money is simply gone. This is what people mean when they say they'd rather pay themselves than pay a landlord. Equity is an asset, and if you manage it correctly, it builds up over time. If you face a huge medical or college tuition bill, you can tap that equity by using a home equity loan or line of credit.

The simple fact is that financially successful Americans buy and own the homes in which they live. It is a significant contributor to their wealth even now, in the wake of the bubble's bursting. The average net worth of a family that owned a home in 2013 was $783,000 (a median of $195,000), compared with an average net worth of $70,000 for renters (a median of just $5,400), according to the Federal Reserve's *Survey of Consumer Finances*, which is published every three years. Those figures tell the story. To own a home is to be worth more. We know this fact in our gut, and when you poll Americans, they say that the most valuable long-term investment is real estate. They say this even when the stock market posts double-digit year-to-year gains. According to a recent Gallup Poll, 31 percent of Americans say housing is the most valuable investment they know of. It's no wonder Americans feel this way. The truth is, buying a home in an area you are already familiar with gives you a knowledge advantage that you simply can't replicate in other parts of your investing life, such as buying stocks or bonds. Chances are that you already know what parts of town are considered safe and good investments. This edge is critical.

There are other solid financial reasons for investing in a primary home, and many involve taxes:

- The mortgage interest deduction is the biggest tax break most families use, and it reportedly saves taxpayers as much as $100 billion each year. You'll have to itemize your taxes to get the benefit, but if you do, you'll be able to reduce your reportable income to the IRS by the amount you paid in interest on any loan to buy, build, or make improvements to your residence. The amount of deductible mortgage interest you pay is reported each year by your mortgage company on Form 1098. The break is most valuable to new buyers in the early years of a mortgage since amortization schedules assign the highest interest payments to the early years of a loan. The mortgage deduction is one of many that were placed on phased-out schedules at higher income limits under the American Taxpayer Relief Act of 2012. Thank you, President Obama! Phaseouts start at $250,000 of income for singles and $300,000 for couples. The change doesn't eliminate the deduction for most filers, but it does reduce it.

- Uncle Sam also lets you exclude gains of as much as $250,000 for singles and $500,000 for couples from capital gains taxes when you sell your house as long as you purchase a new house for the same amount or more within two years. That means you probably will be able to protect any gains from the sale of your house from the tax man. There are limits, however. You have to have lived in your home for two of the last five years, and the home has to be your main residence.

• Interest on home equity debt is also tax-deductible up to $100,000 for couples. Home equity debt comes in two flavors: the standard home equity loan, in which you borrow in a lump sum, and lines of credit, in which you borrow smaller sums as you need them up to a certain fixed amount. Interest on both is deductible when you itemize your taxes.

Buying and living in your own home makes financial sense because despite everything—the market sell-off and the federal policy misfires—owning a home and investing in it still allows you to grow your wealth. Not only can you increase your equity over time via your payments, upgrades, and (fingers crossed) appreciation, you also get some tasty tax advantages. I believe that you can't let your life be run by misguided ninnies in Washington who don't learn from the past. It's up to you and you alone to find a way to improve your financial base and grow your wealth. Buying a home is one important way to do that.

STARTING YOUR SEARCH

We live differently than our parents did. We move more often, and we don't buy and hold for decades upon decades. For that reason, we have to be much savvier when it comes to buying a home. The stakes in choosing the right property to invest in are higher than ever because people stay in their homes an average of just nine years, according to the American Housing Survey. In other words, these days housing is more of a medium-term investment than a long-term one. That means that if you make a mistake, time isn't on your side. Covering up mistakes becomes difficult because you won't have 30 years of appreciation to make up for a misstep. Keep in mind too that the homes you're likely to encounter when you buy may have few, if any, of the features on your wish list. The average home in this country was built 30 years ago, and its architects could not have anticipated our desire for open floor plans and light-filled rooms or the fact that many homes now accommodate multiple generations. No pressure here, but picking the right home in the first place is probably the most important decision you will make to guarantee that it becomes a foundation of your rising wealth. Price, too, is critical. Pay too much and you may never get back your original investment. The condition of the house matters greatly too. Pick a house with problems and you may be forced to spend a huge amount of money on renovations and repairs.

Most of us make the mistake of starting our search for a house by going to big real estate websites such as Zillow .com and Trulia.com. You should start by knowing what you can afford so that you can be realistic about the houses you look at. If a large house with five bedrooms and three baths doesn't fit your budget, you're setting yourself up for frustration. The first step in buying a home is understanding what you can afford. This is a simple calculation: you shouldn't spend more than 33 percent of your gross income on housing. In other words, if you make $100,000, your limit for housing per year should be $33,000, or $2,750 a month. Moreover, it's up to you to know what you can afford. Realtors are happy to push you to upgrade your budget without concerning themselves with whether you'll be able to afford groceries. And if you have good credit, lenders are happy to have you spend every last dime on housing. In fact, not too long ago I contacted a lender in a vacation home market I had been investigating. After looking at our financials, the lending agent offered to lend us $1 million. I had no intention of borrowing a million dollars—or even half that. My husband and I had a much more modest budget in mind, particularly since we intended to pay most of the cost of the home in cash. But buyer beware! If you are a good credit risk, you may be offered more than you want. Don't take the bait.

Once you know what you can afford, you'll want to assess what you can get for your money. First things first. At this writing, inventories of homes are down. In short, more home buyers will be competing for fewer homes in the marketplace. This will make the process of buying more stressful. Of course, the devil is in the details, and although the inventory shortfall may be the national story, market dynamics may be different where you are looking. That makes it all the more important to get good information on your local market. In many communities, the local association of Realtors has a website where it posts its reports on how many homes are selling and at what price. This can be a great reservoir of information that goes a critical step beyond the big retail sites that tell you what sellers want but not what they get for their abodes. If there is not one of these websites available to you, it makes sense to contact a Realtor active in your neighborhood or the neighborhood you want to buy in for information. Two numbers are critical: price per square foot and days on the market.

To get a sense of how much you should pay for any specific property, divide the average sale price of homes sold over the last six to nine months (which you can get from the Realtor's report) by the house's total square footage. This will give you a yardstick, or a rule of thumb, by which to evaluate properties you think fit your budget. If the price per square foot is significantly higher than the average, the property is overpriced. If the opposite is the case, it's underpriced. This isn't the last word on price, by the way, because the terms of housing deals typically are set three months before they are made public. The other important number is what Realtors call days on the market. You can get this benchmark from a local Realtor. As you might expect, it's simply the number of days it takes the average home to sell. According to the National Association of Realtors, that number nationally was 95 days at this writing. (You can find a more up-to-date number at Realtor.com). However, the days-on-market statistic for Dallas, Denver, and Washington was virtually half the national average, whereas Pittsburgh and Cleveland were well over that. You'll want to find out how long any property you are considering seriously has been on the market. A listing that is older offers more opportunity for negotiation. Watch for homes that are being listed a second time. This is often evidence of a troubled listing or simply a house that was mispriced the first time around.

If you are shopping in a neighborhood or city that is new to you, you'll want to get a sense of the health of that community. Communities are like people: some are healthy and thriving, and others are not. Check out the employment situation by talking to neighbors or reading newspapers. Check out the common attributes for homes in your price range. Do they all have renovated kitchens? Two-car garages?

You'll want to narrow your search to houses that have those features—and more, preferably. I believe the best way to shop is to put together a list of your must-have attributes, such as access to good schools, your desired number of bedrooms, and any other absolutes, such as outdoor recreational space. Then, as you look, you can keep detailed notes on the properties that fill that bill and the ones that don't.

In all likelihood you'll choose a Realtor to help you find the perfect fit. At a minimum you'll want someone with experience in the neighborhood in which you're conducting your search. Agents are obligated to pass on any pertinent information about a deal, such as offers from rivals and details about sellers they may have gleaned, including their timetables; this is all information that can be critical to negotiating your deal successfully. They also have to maintain your confidentiality. Keep in mind that most real estate agents work on commission: that's an agent's fee for service. Sellers pay them that commission, usually 6 percent, though it can vary, and negotiate it as part of the listing agreement. The commission then is split between the seller's listing broker and your agent (the selling agent). A good agent does a quick study of your needs and directs you to properties that fit those parameters. Agents can answer broad questions about a community such as school district boundaries and the all-important days-on-market statistic, but also should know details such as quirky home owner association rules that place a limit on the number of pets you own. Unfortunately, the real estate business is rife with conflicts of interest. A common one facing buyers is dual agency, which occurs when a single agent represents both buyer and seller. This kind of arrangement is most typical in small markets where there are few agents. But you should understand the risks before agreeing to work with an agent who also represents the buyer. Remember, the seller is paying the commission, and that means the pressure on the agent will be high to raise any offer you make on a house. One way to get around this problem is to use an exclusive buyer's agent, a sales pro who represents only buyers. You can find exclusive buyer's agents at the website of the National Association of Exclusive Buyer Agents.

Before you settle on an agent, interview that person to make sure he or she is familiar with the neighborhood you've settled on and works full-time. Members of the National Association of Realtors are bound to follow a code of ethics that requires them to pass along pertinent information to buyers. I've worked with terrific agents who are on top of every new listing in a marketplace and regularly update their clients with information about new listings that fit their needs, as well as those agents who sit back on their haunches and wait for the client to do the work. You want someone who is motivated to help you get the deal done. The last thing you want is to have your search falter because your agent isn't proactive. Be sure to talk to people the agent has represented recently. A good reference from someone you know and trust is truly valuable. A word about managing your agent during the search: if you are looking for a home with a partner, designate one person to communicate with the agent. That way you'll be less likely to send mixed messages.

The postcrash market means that there are still huge numbers of home owners who are sitting on their houses because they still owe more than their mortgage loans are worth. In other words, if they were to sell, they'd have to pay the bank a substantial sum rather than cashing in, as they have no equity in the house. As you search, you may encounter people who've been eager to sell for some time and are only now able to unload their biggest investment. An eager seller is always good for buyers, but you may find that those sellers have less flexibility on selling prices.

FINDING A RELIABLE LENDER

Even as you shop for a house, you'll want to get your financing lined up. That process starts with choosing a mortgage lender that offers competitive rates and that you feel comfortable dealing with. Having your financing set up can give you a competitive edge over other buyers. Sellers consider buyers who have gone to the trouble of doing this as more serious and view their offers more favorably. Besides, the first home you look at may be the one you end up offering to buy.

The lending business has changed a lot in the last few years. The good news is that if you are getting into the market for the first time or just for the first time in a long while, the fundamentals are the same—and are straightforward. At its simplest a mortgage is a loan that makes up the difference between the down payment you are making on your home and the purchase price. If you're buying a $250,000 house and putting down 20 percent, or $50,000, your mortgage covers the difference: $200,000. Unlike other types of loans, mortgages use real estate as collateral. That means that if you fail to make the monthly payments, the bank has the right to take your home from you. A mortgage has a term or length, usually 15 or 30 years. The rule of thumb is to take out the shortest-term mortgage you can afford because the longer the payment period is, the more you pay in interest over time. Consider a borrower with $200,000 in debt. If that borrower had taken out a 30-year fixed-rate mortgage at 5 percent and made every single one of the 360 payments of $1,073.64, he or she would have ended up paying a total of $386,511.57, or $186,511.57 in interest! Yet if that borrower had cut the term to 15 years, he or she would have paid a total of $284,685.71, or $84,685.71 in interest. The savings here are impressive: $101,825.86 over the 30-year mortgage. (You can run your own numbers at Interest.com.) Of course, many people refinance or swap out of their loans long before their terms end.

That's where the similarities between the premeltdown mortgage world and the postmeltdown mortgage world end.

I believe the business of mortgage lending has changed even more than the housing market itself has. Two big things have changed. First, federal rules regarding mortgages have been tightened. Second, because of the rule changes as well as the fines and fees extracted from the industry that we described earlier, there are fewer lenders willing to make mortgage loans. As a result, the nation's largest banks have significantly scaled back their mortgage operations. Much of the business now is handled by banks that aren't really banks. According to the American Enterprise Institute, big banks held a 61 percent market share in 2012, but by 2015 that share had fallen to 33 percent. Nonbanks have picked up the slack and now make 51 percent of loans. One of those is Quicken Loans. That company is the biggest online lender in the country and the largest player in the market for government-backed loans. Quicken is not a bank but one of the many nonbanks that make loans every single day. My advice: don't shy away. New upstarts in the business are giving out the best deals.

Tighter mortgage rules will mean that qualifying will be more difficult and finding a lender more complicated. As part of Dodd-Frank, the Consumer Financial Protection Bureau has set in place tougher standards for consumers to prove they can repay their loans. Lenders have to look at current income, employment status, and estimated monthly mortgage payments as well as debt-to-income ratios, which must be 43 percent or less. Lenders no longer are allowed to offer loans with negative amortization (your debt rises even as you meet the loan payment requirements), and generally only 3 percent of the total loan amount can be charged for points and fees. The latter is a good thing, certainly, but the unintended consequence of these new rules (which I am giving you only a taste of) is that it has sent a chill through the lending industry. Some banks have stayed in the business, but others have gotten out altogether or reduced the size of their mortgage businesses. You can find lenders in your area by going to Bankrate.com or HSH.com.

Finding a lender is like tracking down a real estate agent or a contractor. Start by asking friends and family members for recommendations. A respected real estate agent is another place to turn for suggestions. Check out Internet players, your credit union, and any local small or midsize banks. The more offers you can compare, the better chance you have of finding the best deal possible. Whether it's a credit union or a bank, the best place to get started is where you have your checking account right now. Check out local rates on its website as well as on HSH.com and Bankrate.com. You may not qualify for these rates, but at least you'll be able to determine which institutions have the most competitive offers on interest rates.

Now, go online to a website that brings a number of lenders to the table, such as LendingTree.com or eloan.com. These sites are lead generators for banks. Be careful about how much personal information you share with these sites, but by spending a little time filling out forms, you fairly quickly can come up with mortgage offers to see whether they are more attractive than the ones you were able to find from your own contacts. If you conduct a mortgage search efficiently, inquiries into your credit report won't affect your credit score.

Like many other businesses, mortgage lending is run by software programs. Forget the old green eyeshade–sporting accountants crunching numbers late into the night. These days whether you get a loan comes down to whether an auto-mated underwriting program deems you worthy. These pro-grams consider income, how long you have been in your job, and, most important, your credit score to determine how much of a lending risk you are. Although the debt ratio men-tioned earlier in this chapter is important to you in determin-ing how much you should spend, lenders base their decision on how much to lend you on how well you've managed credit in the past. A credit score does just that. Scores can range from the 300s to 900. If you have a score of 700 or higher, you'll be given wide latitude in borrowing. A score below 650 will give you rates well above the advertised ones. You can check out your credit reports for free at AnnualCreditReport .com. You can purchase one of the most widely used scores, the FICO or Fair Isaac Corporation, score at myFICO.com.

One of the key decisions you'll make as you choose a lender and get preapproved for a mortgage is just what flavor of mortgage you want. Generally, there are fewer different types of loans in the wake of the crash. The government has put the kibosh on 40-year loans (mortgage loans that extended over 40 years rather than 30 or 15, resulting in exorbitant interest charges), and subprime loans aren't as readily available as they once were. However, you'll still have the option of choosing between a 15-year and a 30-year-fixed-rate mortgage, what I call a plain vanilla loan, and a host of adjustable loans. Adjustable loans start out with a low teaser rate and then rise over time. I'll address how to pick the right loan in the section titled "Managing Your Equity" later in this chapter.

In sum, the mortgage market has changed dramatically in the wake of the recession and the housing meltdown. Although conservatives decry the loosening of lending standards by housing administrators, lending is still below market highs because banks are still so cautious in lending money. Stingy bankers can make it difficult to buy your dream home, and unfortunately, this has coincided with a period in which income has largely been stagnant. In fact, between 2012 and 2014, housing prices rose 13 times faster than did wages. According to a study from RealtyTrac, 141 of 184 metro areas saw housing price gains outpace wage hikes for the period, and 45 of those metro areas saw median home prices spike past 28 percent of median income for monthly mortgage payments. That's pretty much the baseline beyond which housing is considered unaffordable. Even so, prices remain below the highs of the market. The lesson for buyers is to make sure your credit report is in the best shape

possible. Contest errors in the report and be sure to be dili-
gent about meeting due dates on bills you owe as you shop.

FINDING THE RIGHT INVESTMENT

I could have titled this section "Finding the Right House,"
but I want you to keep in mind that what you're buying is
an investment. Even as you shop, you'll want to think about
what might appeal to other buyers when you get ready to sell
years down the road. In other words, you're going to have to
keep your eyes on practical matters as you search. Getting
distracted by a charming garden or attractive furnishings
will prevent you from basing a decision on key fundamentals such as whether the house is well constructed, is in
good shape, and has good bones. You'll need to evaluate the
neighborhood in which the house is situated. Is it close to
employment centers, good schools, and services you'll need
as you go about your day-to-day activities, such as conve-
nient grocery stores and doctors? Two factors are critical:
schools and property taxes. Good schools are key to home
values. Although fewer and fewer households are made up of
the traditional family unit of two parents and two children,
it pays to buy in neighborhoods with top-notch schools.
If you're new to an area, contact high schools directly in
towns that have drawn your interest. They'll provide free

self-evaluations that describe students' performance on SAT tests, the number of advanced placement courses offered, and other data that should help you evaluate their performance. Yes, student-teacher ratios are important, but they are not the only number you should weigh. Although most schools are happy to share graduation rates, you should ask about dropout rates as well. When my husband and I were shopping for a home, we could have bought in any one of three states. Narrowing our search was difficult. Fortunately, there are websites that can help. SchoolDigger.com, for example, gives you access to test scores and student-teacher ratios for free at the touch of a mouse.

Another critical factor is property taxes. You'd think that with the decline in housing prices, property taxes would be falling like a stone. No way. Property tax collections continue to rise, and the highest are eye-popping. According to Zillow.com, Westchester County in New York State has the highest average property taxes in the nation at $13,842 a year. That's more than six times the national average tax bill of $2,132. Notice of higher tax rates typically is made in the fall each year, and with a little elbow grease you can find out whether higher taxes are in the offing. There are two key factors to understand: the home's assessed value and your millage rate, or the amount of money you owe per thousand dollars of property value. Towns and cities that wish to raise taxes can decide to reassess properties (and therefore raise their assessed value) or boost your millage rate. Either way, before you buy into a neighborhood, you'll want to know if a tax hike is on the horizon.

Once you've narrowed your search, you'll want to spend more time on the ground in the neighborhoods you've targeted. Visit at different times of the day and week. Being on-site during a busy afternoon rush hour can tell you which streets become shortcuts for commuters. Don't forget to visit on weekends to find out whether parents are confident enough to allow their children to play outside on their own. The more time you spend on the ground, the better sense you'll get of the neighborhood and whether it's right for you and your family.

When you finally find the perfect house, you'll want to make a home inspection a condition of purchase. During the dot-com boom in San Francisco, my husband and I spent hours looking at homes in the Bay Area. As a way to get an edge in the frenetic bidding wars that went on there, buyers routinely would drop home inspection as a contingency of closing the deal. It was a mistake. A good home inspector can see things you probably won't. Is the effervescence on the basement walls a sign of water damage or is there nothing to worry about? Does the house need a major electrical upgrade? Is the roof safe or on the verge of needing replacement? These are the questions you'll need a pro to sort out so that you can make a solid investment.

Because some states have no requirements for inspectors,

you'll want to start your search for an inspector with professional organizations. The American Society of Home Inspectors (ASHI) requires that its fully accredited members pass a written exam and have a minimum of 250 home inspections under their belts. To stave off any conflicts of interest, the organization's code of ethics prohibits inspectors from doing any contracting work on a home within one year of the inspection.

A home inspection should follow the standards of procedure laid out by ASHI. Typically it is a three-hour process in which the inspector examines the structural and mechanical condition of the house. The inspector will examine the heating, cooling, electrical, and plumbing systems as well as the foundation. A good overview of what is covered can be found at the website ASHI.org, where you also can find a virtual house inspection tool that details common problems. Just as important as what is covered is what is not. The inspection typically doesn't cover mold, and the inspector is not required to look for termites, though he or she will look for wood damage. As a buyer, you want to be present at the inspection because a good inspector will give you a lesson in maintenance on the house as well as a tour of its workings. He or she can show you the water shutoff valves and describe the workings of the furnace as well as the routine maintenance it requires. He or she can tell you whether the electrical box is adequate or below standard.

A home inspector once kept my husband and me from

buying a dangerous money pit. The two of us had found a charming farmhouse in rural northern Westchester County that we immediately fell in love with. The white clapboard farmhouse was rambling because of an addition, but it was set on a beautiful piece of property with a stone fence surrounding it. The property even had a small playhouse designed to mimic the original home right down to the black shutters with quarter-moon cutouts. As we drove up to the house, we were entranced. Tom Kraeutler, a longtime inspector and host of *The Money Pit* radio show, whom I had hired to inspect the house, drove up behind us. An attractive young woman, the owner, strode out of the front door with a black Lab at her heels. At that point, my husband and I diverged. He walked toward the owner and her real estate agent, and Tom and I went to the back of the house to start looking the place over. We started with the exterior. Tom took a flathead screwdriver and ran it along one of the seams of the siding, applying gentle but firm pressure. The head of the tool plunged in. I watched as he shook his head. A fuller examination revealed that water damage was causing rot all along the exterior of the home. I shuddered at the thought of the cost of replacing all that wooden siding. All this had taken less than five minutes, and already I knew I wasn't going to buy the house. Inside, though, my husband was being charmed by the real estate agent and the owner. As it turned out, the damaged siding wasn't the only problem. We eventually trekked to the basement to get a look at the furnace. A low ceiling had all of us hunched over to get a good view, and it was a doozy. The red-hot pipes leading away from the furnace were mere inches from the wooden ceiling beams, which were so dry that they were flaking—a likely fire hazard. Tom rolled his eyes and began to speak about the trouble with the design. By that time, both my husband and I knew there was no way we were going to buy that house.

One of the reasons Tom was so effective was that we chose him ourselves. Be aware of the conflicts of interest that routinely plague this business. Home inspectors rely on agents for business, and agents routinely recommend the inspectors who are most likely to give a home a clean bill of health. To make sure that your inspector isn't under the thumb of real estate agents, talk to buyers the inspector has worked with before. Find someone you like and give that person repeat business yourself. Having a pro like Tom whose loyalty is to you and your welfare at your side is invaluable. Again, be sure to attend the inspection yourself. There's no substitute for seeing everything firsthand.

NEGOTIATING THE DEAL

Negotiating the price of a house—again, probably the biggest investment of your life—can be intimidating. The problem is that there is no one simple strategy that works.

The first step—choosing the initial offering bid—is the most important. Set it too high and you can't go back. Set it too low and you could lose out on a gem. This is where knowing the numbers is essential. As we talked about earlier, check out the comparables in the neighborhood—those price-per-square-foot numbers we talked about—and apply that statistic to the total square footage of the house. That's a great starting point for a bid. How long has the house has been on the market? The longer the seller has been holding on to the home, the antsier he or she will be to sell. Also, the seller's real estate agent will be motivated to make a deal if she or he has been marketing the house for months. Contracts typically specify a time frame. Most last only 90 days. As time goes by, pressure increases for the agent to generate a sale before the seller decides to move on to another agent.

As the agents say, all real estate is local, and so as part of your research you also want to know whether the neighborhood of the house you're bidding on is red hot, stone cold, or something in between. In a red-hot market, watch for agents who try to encourage bidding wars. This scenario in all likelihood is a losing proposition for bidders. Avoid seller agents who want to rush the negotiations because that is when you have the most leverage. Remember, sellers need you at the negotiating table. If a market is cool or cold, consider asking for concessions or even make a lowball offer. Some sellers may be willing to lose some profit if they have locked in big gains since they bought the house. Alternatively, sellers who accept a lowball offer may be trying to unload a home in poor condition.

Flexibility can be another way to get your offer chosen. Often buyers are under some sort of time pressure to sell. Maybe they are retiring and already have bought their dream home at the beach. Rather than foot two mortgages, they want to sell quickly. Or maybe the kids need to get started in the new school district before the new school year gets under way. Either way, if you can move quickly, that can make your offer more appealing. Finally, if a deal is keeping you up nights, it isn't for you. By this point, you should have a solid enough understanding of what you can afford and what the market will bear to feel comfortable with any offer you are making. Keep in mind the long-term appeal of the house as it is today and as you'd like to see it—whether that appeal makes sense for you and the future families that will own it.

CLOSING THE DEAL

I can tell you authoritatively that closing on a home is one of the most anxiety-provoking experiences you will ever have. In most states, it is an hours-long process in which you are required to sign stacks of documents, almost none of which you will have time to read. Closing costs are rising, up 5.7 percent in 2014 from the previous year, and the average paid on a $200,000 mortgage is $2,539. The costs are rising because after the housing bust regulators decided to require lenders to do more due diligence on borrowers to make sure they could pay. Those costs were passed on directly to buyers. (You can thank the Consumer Financial Protection Bureau for that one.) Your lender will have estimated the closing fees you'll be paying in your good-faith estimate. You'll want to check that estimate against actual costs, which will be detailed in a document called the HUD-1 form. Also, don't take any guff from lawyers. When I asked for the HUD-1 form from *my own attorney* before the close on our home, she tried to turn me down! It's your right to check your fees, and the only way to do it is to get the right documentation. The fees fall into three camps: set fees, often going to third parties such as appraisers; fees that are going to the lender and fattening its profit; and prepaid fees such as one year of property taxes. Fees going to third parties shouldn't be different from the good-faith estimate provided. If they are markedly different, ask questions. The fees that are most easily negotiated are lender-charged fees, including charges for application, origination, commitment, loan discount, and broker and underwriting fees. Get creative. Don't just ask that the fee be waived. You might, for example, suggest that any application fee you are being asked to pay be credited toward the closing costs.

MANAGING YOUR EQUITY

The bottom line when it comes to your home isn't the bricks and mortar; as I said earlier, that, in all likelihood, belongs to your lender. What you own—your true wealth—is your equity. And that equity needs one thing: managing.

To reiterate, home equity is whatever payments toward the principal you have made, your down payment, and any appreciation from gains that the market has given you or that you have earned with home improvements. If prices have declined instead of rising, that's a negative input into your calculation. Say you bought a $500,000 house three years ago and put $100,000 down and took out a $400,000 loan. Right off the bat you have $100,000 in equity. Fast-forward three years. Your 30-year $400,000 mortgage secured with a 6.5 percent fixed interest rate has you making payments of $2,528. Over those 36 months, you've built up another $14,331 of equity. Let's say you've been lucky and home prices have appreciated 15 percent so that the house would sell at $575,000, a full $75,000 more than you paid for it. Total equity from your down payment, payments on the principal, and appreciation after three years: $189,331. Not too shabby. (Of course, equity can take far longer to grow, particularly if prices are flat or falling in your area.)

Equity is important because it gives you both options and protections. Tapping your equity with a home equity loan or line of credit, for example, can fund a bathroom renovation or pay off expensive credit card debt. Keep in mind that you don't want to go nuts here. By leveraging your home, you are putting it at risk. Make sure your income is secure before proceeding. But you get the picture: equity is an asset you can control and use to your advantage. When it comes time to sell your house, the equity you've built up ensures that you will be able to pay off the mortgage with the proceeds from the sale even if the market takes a dip. Of course, confidence isn't just about scraping by. Your house should return a healthy profit whether you plan to live in it for 13 years or 30.

Unfortunately, many Americans continue to be underwater on their loans, which is to say they owe more than the house is worth. This prevents them from taking advantage of their equity. Lenders don't write home equity loans for borrowers who are underwater. What's more, if you sell the house, you'll have to make up the difference between the purchase price and what you owe. Ultimately, for many of these home owners time is the only solution. If you don't sell, you don't have to take those losses and your property has a chance to increase in value over time.

Equity is straightforward, but managing it is far from simple. First, let's calculate that equity. The first figure you need is your payments to the loan's principal. It sounds simple, right? It's just the sum of all your mortgage payments, right? The hard truth is no, it isn't. Your payments to principal are just a portion of that total. Most of your monthly payments, particularly in the early years of a loan, are earmarked to pay interest costs. That proportion changes over time until the last years of your loan, when most of your payments go directly to the principal. For example, on a 30-year fixed-rate loan of $300,000 with a rate of 6.4 percent, just $276.52 of your first mortgage payment of $1,876.52 goes to paying down the principal. The rest, or $1,600.00, goes to paying the interest costs. It's not until the nineteenth year of the mortgage that the situation reverses—more of your monthly payment goes to principal than to interest. To determine just how much of your payments have been going to principal, go to Bankrate.com and navigate to "Mortgage Calculator." If you enter the terms of your loan, including rate of interest, amount financed, and term of repayment, the calculator will show you the portion of your monthly mortgage payment going to principal for each month. Add up all those payments for however long you've had the loan. You also can check your monthly statement through your lender.

Home prices, whether they are rising or falling, can make a huge difference in your wealth. If you live in an area where prices improve at a slow rate, which is typical of much of the Midwest, for example, your wealth from your home also will grow slowly. If you live in a market with a strong local economy such as San Francisco or Miami, the rate of growth can tick along at a furious pace, taking your equity with it.

Just as appreciation can be a tremendous boon to your wealth, depreciation can be a drag on your bottom line.

Declining values can make it difficult or impossible to refinance or pull equity out of your home for other purposes. Naturally, this can make it tough to sell. Thomas and his partner, Josh, had spent hours improving their quaint New Jersey bungalow, investing a total of $60,000, but when Josh unexpectedly received a dream job offer on the West Coast, the two were stuck. Prices had fallen 8 percent in one year in their neighborhood. There was no way they could recoup their investment in the house. They finally decided to rent their home until the market rebounded, but the decision was painful. If prices had not fallen, or "corrected," they would have been able to sell and collect a profit.

Figuring out what gains you've achieved through appreciation can be as simple as calling an appraiser and paying $300 or so for a formal appraisal. You also can estimate those gains on your own for free. If you worked with a real estate agent in buying your house, call the agent and ask for the appreciation rates in your area. Ask specifically how much prices have gone up or down in your town or county each year since you bought the home.

In addition to appreciation and principal payments, you'll want to calculate the contribution to equity made by any upgrades. Whether you've gutted and replaced the kitchen or added a master suite, you've improved your investment and boosted your equity. That's the good news. What most people don't realize, however, is that the return on your investment isn't 100 percent. In other words, you don't get back $1 for every $1 you spend. Your returns depend on how popular the renovation is. Go to www.remodeling.hw.net to see what buyers in your area would pay for the improvements you've made.

Now that you have all the elements you need to calculate how much equity you have in your home, getting the final number is simple: just add your principal payments, your down payment, any appreciation, and any contribution from upgrades and subtract any outstanding mortgage balance or home equity loans. This is the wealth you've accumulated in your home and what you'll want to nurture, grow, and protect. You'll be able to tap it in the event of an emergency—to pay for a new roof if your old one collapses or to pay medical bills if someone in your family gets sick. It probably will be the source of some of the money you might use for upgrades to the house and what you'll use to pay the commission of the real estate agent who sells your home.

Savvy home owners try to grow their equity above and beyond what they would get from the calculation we just made. The mortgage you choose can be critical, and although lenders aren't underwriting some of the wacky loans that they did during the housing boom (NINJA, anyone?), you still need to take particular care about which mortgage you choose because of its impact on your equity. For example, when Alison and Andy decided to buy their home, the young couple had only $12,000 in savings to put down and plenty of college debt. They knew they would have to stretch to buy a home in their area, where prices had been rising consistently. When they found the three-bedroom home of their dreams priced at $320,000, they decided to take the leap, using some creative financing to qualify for a loan. By opting for an adjustable-rate loan that allowed them to pay interest only for most of the debt and then simultaneously taking out a second mortgage—a home equity line of credit—they just managed to qualify for their loan. However, interest rates rose dramatically, pushing their monthly payments $155 higher for the home equity line of credit. Worse, they knew that in just two short years the interest on the first mortgage would reset higher as well. Alison worried about the fact that they were making no headway on their loan, since they were making interest-only payments. The burden of their $1,800 monthly mortgage payment seemed heavier each month. Fortunately, Alison's parents stepped in and gave them some financial help until they could refinance into a 30-year fixed-rate loan. If they had encountered a real financial emergency, they could have faced foreclosure.

It's doubtful that any lender today would make such a risky "piggyback" loan, and interest-only mortgage options have virtually disappeared from the marketplace. But you get the picture: lenders aren't really concerned about whether you're growing equity. It's up to you to make sure you're picking the best loan to do that. Thirty-year or 15-year fixed-rate loans are the best option for that goal. Loans with an adjustable rate for a set period at the start of the mortgage

loan aren't as good because of your exposure to higher interest rates over time. Higher rates mean more money into the
lender's pocket and more money out of yours.

Even after you choose a good mortgage, you'll want to
track mortgage rates periodically to make sure you're paying
the lowest rates possible. The rate of interest you pay on your
loan is critical to building wealth because the more you pay in
interest, the less you have available for paying the principal.
Even a difference of a point and a half can mean a lot to your
monthly payment. If you have a 30-year fixed-rate loan for
$250,000 financed at 6 percent, you could cut your monthly
payments by $232 if you refinanced the loan at 4.5 percent.
For that reason, you'll want to keep a sharp eye on mortgage
rates at all times. An easy way to do that is to check websites
such as Bankrate.com and HSH.com, where you'll see not
just the nationally advertised rates but the rates for your area.
(Keep in mind that you'll be viewing rates for the applicants
with the best credit scores.) A refinance can help you make
the most of falling rates by getting a cheaper mortgage or roll-
ing a 30-year mortgage and a high-rate second mortgage into
one low-rate loan. It used to be that for a refinance to make
financial sense there had to be a 2-percentage-point difference between the rate you could get and the rate you currently had, but automation of loans has made it possible to
get a good deal when the difference is smaller. A good rule
of thumb to follow is to consider refinancing when mortgage
rates drop 1 full percentage point below your loan's rate.

Refinancing is not free, however, and it's not for everyone. You'll face thousands of dollars in closing costs when you refinance, including application fees, credit check fees (yes, you pay for that), attorney fees, and title insurance; the list goes on and on. If you have a 30-year loan and are 10 years into that loan, you probably don't want to consider refinancing into another 30-year loan because you would end up paying enormous interest costs on the remainder of the loan balance. A person in that situation may well want to consider refinancing into a 15-year-loan, although the payment per month will be higher, because of the reduced interest costs over the life of the loan. Finally, although a refinance can result in impressive monthly savings, the home mortgage deduction on your yearly taxes will drop because you'll be paying less in interest. To determine how much you'll lose in tax savings, multiply your savings by your federal tax rate. For example, if you stand to save $400 each month and are in the 33 percent tax bracket, you'll lose tax savings of $132 monthly, for a net saving of $268 a month.

To determine how long it will take to break even on your refinance, follow this simple formula: add up the refinance fees and divide the total by your after-tax monthly savings on the refinance. The result? The number of months it will take until you break even. For example, using the figures above, if the refinance fees were $6,300, the break-even point would be 23 months, or nearly 2 years. Remember, if your break-even period is longer than the amount of time you intend to live in the home, skip the refinance because it won't be worth it.

Most people don't realize that their home equity line of credit also can be refinanced. With more people taking out these loans, it makes sense to keep this in mind. Because they have variable rates of interest, these loans can become expensive quickly. Calculating whether it makes sense to refinance is easy. Here's how to calculate a blended rate of interest. Let's say you have total mortgage debt of $300,000, $200,000 of which is a first mortgage financed at a rate of 6.5 percent. The remainder is a home equity line of credit (HELOC) with an outstanding balance of $100,000 at 8 percent. Divide your first mortgage amount ($200,000) by the total ($300,000) and multiply by the interest rate (6.5 percent) for a total of 4.33 percent. Next divide the outstanding HELOC balance ($100,000) by the total debt ($300,000) and multiply by your rate (8.0 percent) for a total of 2.67. Add the two rates together (7.0 percent). This is the rate you'll have to beat to make sure the deal is worthwhile.

Another way to build equity is simply to pay down the mortgage faster. With your actual interest costs totaling hundreds of thousands of dollars over the life of the loan, it's no wonder that plenty of people advocate paying down a mortgage as quickly as possible. After all, if you have a 30-year fixed-rate mortgage for $250,000 at 7 percent, you'll end up paying total interest of $348,772 by the end of the mortgage term. In reality, you'll want to consider several issues before throwing every last nickel at your mortgage. First, determine whether your current mortgage has a prepayment penalty; such fees can run into the thousands of dollars. Keep in mind, too, that to the degree you pay down your mortgage, you'll significantly cut into your mortgage interest deduction. A reasonable way to prepay is to make one additional mortgage payment a year. By adding just one additional payment, you'll significantly cut into the loan balance. This is most easily done by adding a twelfth of a payment to each regular monthly payment or by adding an extra payment during one of the months with five weeks. Some people get so carried away trying to erase their mortgage debt that they shortchange their retirement savings. That's a bad idea.

If you put less than 20 percent down when you bought the house, you may be paying private mortgage insurance (PMI), a policy that reimburses the lenders if you default on your mortgage. Most lenders require PMI until your loan-to-value ratio drops below 80 percent. Simply put, the loan-to-value ratio is the ratio of your loan size to the appraised value of your house. If you have a loan of $250,000 on a home with a value of $275,000, you have a 90 percent loan-to-value ratio, calculated by dividing $250,000 by $275,000. As you make payments, obviously your loan size falls; appreciation also can boost the value. After a few years, you probably don't technically have to have private mortgage insurance. Lenders are required to cancel PMI once you pay your loan balance down to 78 percent of the home's original appraised value, but you can ask that it be removed at 80 percent. Check your mortgage servicer's annual statement to find a contact to request PMI cancellation.

Another way to protect your investment in your home is to make sure you don't overimprove the house. To be sure, you'll spend thousands of dollars maintaining your home—painting the interior and exterior and repairing the roof—but when it comes to upgrades you don't want to own the Taj Mahal on a street full of ranches. As you consider what projects to pursue, remember that only a handful of projects pay for themselves dollar for dollar. On average, renovations return just 62.2 percent of their cost at sale time. Those numbers have weakened as the costs of renovations have risen while home values have stayed low. As was mentioned earlier in this chapter, www.remodeling.hw.net can help you find the renovations that return the most in your part of the country. Of course, the fact that you don't make money on a renovation doesn't mean you shouldn't do it. Renovations still make sense for two important reasons. First, you can't live in a house for 10, 12, or 20 years and not make any changes to it. If you don't maintain your home, your property will lose value. Maintenance doesn't mean just keeping the gutters clean. It also means recognizing the trends that are in demand by home buyers, and it makes your home feel current. The average home is more than 30 years old, and its layout and design offer far less than what most families want today. A home that is kept up to date and is well maintained will sell faster and at a higher premium than will a home that appears neglected. Second and also critically important, these investments aren't like stock certificates that you shove in a bank vault. You and your family will be able to enjoy the investment for years to come.

Still, you'll want to decide how much you intend to spend before you hire a contractor. Knowing your budget limits is as important as setting a budget to buy the house in the first place. Unless your area is gentrifying rapidly, you'll want to limit your renovation budget to 20 percent of your home's value. That means that if you live in a $350,000 house, you'll need to cap your improvement budget at $70,000. There are times this rule can be broken. Clearly, if your area is gentrifying, as was mentioned above, values will be improving over time, and you can spend more. You should also consider the neighborhood. A girlfriend of mine and her husband bought a small carriage house in a tony neighborhood near the ocean. Her house was the smallest in sight but was across the street from the yacht club. She expanded the second floor, renovated the kitchen, and took down walls to open up the first floor. The transformation was stunning. Her budget was a whopping 50 percent of what she paid for the home in the first place. Still, the move made sense because of the value of homes in her neighborhood.

SELLING YOUR HOME

When you decide to sell your home, you'll want to be sure the entire property is in tip-top condition. I can't tell you the number of homes on the market I've been in that smell like dogs or cigarette smoke. Consider staging the home if you've lived in it for more than 10 years. People collect so much stuff over time that it is nearly impossible to see their homes with fresh eyes, but that is exactly what a buyer wants to see: your home without the golf trophy or bass photos. One house I toured contained a 500-piece collection of porcelain Hummel figurines! Remember that your tastes are not everybody's. Take down the personal photos on the wall. Reduce the number of pieces of furniture in each room; less furniture makes a room look bigger. If there is a smoker in the house, have the carpets cleaned and vacuum the upholstered furniture.

Painting interior walls that have been neglected is a great idea. Just don't go crazy with color. Deep hues may be the flavor of the moment, but a neutral cream or white will make the home look clean and well cared for. If the exterior is drab, consider painting the door a bright color such as red. Prune the landscaping and make sure the exterior fixtures work. Few things are as off-putting for a buyer as trying to turn on a light and having nothing happen.

If your home is older, consider upgrading the wiring. It's not sexy, but young and technologically savvy buyers know that their demands for juice are high. A 200-amp panel is the minimum typically, but panel size is governed by the National Electrical Code. Hire a licensed electrician to do the work.

You probably won't want to renovate the kitchen right before selling, but small changes can make a big difference in buyers' perceptions. Make minor repairs such as fixing a leaky faucet and removing the burn marks from the counter-top. Updating cabinet hardware can help, and changing the curtains can spruce up your look for very little money. If your refrigerator, range, or dishwasher is old, consider updating it to drive buyers' interest. Bathrooms can make a bad impression unless they are well maintained and spotless. Regrout tile and remove any metal corrosion on faucets and handles.

Choosing the right Realtor will be critical to getting the most for your home when you sell. After all, you will be facing plenty of bills after the transaction. The biggest one may be the payoff figure for your present loan: how much you still owe on the house. As was noted earlier, you also will pay the broker's commission, any prepayment penalty on your mortgage, and attorney's fees. You also may be asked by your agent or attorney to pay any of the following: title insurance premiums, transfer taxes, survey fees, inspection and repairs, recording fees, home owner association fees, and document preparation.

A good Realtor can help you set the right price, paying particular attention to psychological break points that motivate buyers. Although buyers are notorious for expanding their budgets once they find a home they like, the reality that is they won't even come to see your home if it's priced above their break point. Those break points occur at every $100,000 and then every $25,000. As a seller, you'll want to identify those points and price just a little bit below them to guarantee that the widest possible audience sees your home. A good Realtor will have a sophisticated website that will promote your house to buyers. This is critical because more than 60 percent of buyers use the Web as a search tool. You'll want the web page featuring your home to have a 360-degree view of the house, with pictures that make the most of its best features.

In the best-case scenario, you will be fielding multiple offers on your home, but even that situation can require careful navigation. One way to put yourself firmly in control in a warm to hot market is to give bidders a deadline for submitting bids and open all offers at the same time. This will organize the process and allow you to choose the offer that best matches your needs. Remember, as a seller you are exposed to risk in every part of the deal. If a buyer's financing doesn't come through or you can't come to terms on a settlement date, the deal will fall apart. For that reason, sometimes the highest offer isn't the best.

If your local market is still weak, reducing your asking price is the surest way of sparking interest in your home, but it's not the only way to get a deal done. You also can offer to pay part of the buyer's closing costs or three months' worth of home owner association dues or throw in appliances for buyers who appear to be waffling. The bottom line is that you may need to get creative to get your house sold.

Here's the good news: if you do manage to walk away with a profit, you'll be able to shelter up to $250,000 for singles and $500,000 for couples from the tax man.

BUYING A SECOND HOME

Increasingly, boomers are looking for second homes that they can move to when they retire. The 8,000 boomers who will be retiring every day over the next 15 years are bound to reshape the second home market. Instead of a beachfront home, more boomers are opting to retire in cities and college towns where they have access to museums, free classes, and restaurants and a faster pace of living. Many want a smaller home and less maintenance. It makes sense to start planning for this transition before you retire and while you still have monthly income.

The first thing to consider is the full cost of owning a second home. Sure, there's the monthly mortgage, but ongoing expenses can add up, such as upkeep, insurance, and possibly hiring a management company or a trusted caretaker to look in on the property since you won't be there every day. A home owner on Kiawah Island in South Carolina told me that he never planned on the extensive costs of maintaining the palmetto trees on his property. That cost was thousands of dollars every year! Flood insurance costs need to be taken into consideration for beach and lakefront buyers, and a redrawing of the flood maps by the government may mean higher costs for some.

If you aren't paying all cash for your second home, you'll find banks have higher financial requirements for second-home buyers than for first-home buyers. Typically, you'll need to make a considerable down payment. Some lenders require borrowers to put down 25 percent of the purchase price before writing a mortgage for the balance, and the median down payment in 2013 was 26 percent. Keep in mind that 38 percent of second home buyers will pay all cash. Some folks opt to add a second mortgage, either a home equity line of credit or a home equity loan, to the mortgage for their primary home to pay for the second house. Understand that doing this puts both of your properties at risk of default. Some seniors use a reverse mortgage to tap their home equity, but this strategy, too, has problems since you are essentially handing over your primary home to the bank.

MY LAST WORD ON HOME OWNERSHIP

You probably can tell I am bullish on housing. That's the case because I believe that in the housing market, average Americans have a knowledge advantage that doesn't exist in other markets. In all likelihood, you already know the best neighborhoods, the best school districts, and even the best streets in the area where you live. The same thing can't be said about investing in the stock market. Sure, you can spend a lot of time researching companies, but ultimately, let's face it, you won't be getting the tips that market insiders do. What's more, with a home you'll have time to allow your investment to mature. Housing isn't the only answer to building wealth over time, but it is an important part of the equation.

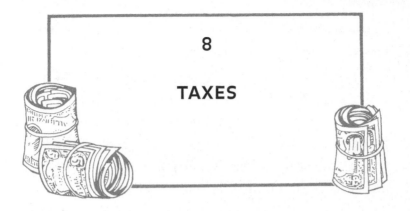

8

TAXES

Imagine getting a letter from the IRS that questions whether you paid what you owe in taxes. The letter is not a full-on audit but a challenge to prove that what you reported is true. Chilling, right? That's exactly what happened to tens of thousands of small-business owners the IRS suspected might have underpaid their tax bills in recent years. However, the agency didn't have the hard proof required to conduct an actual audit. "Your gross receipts *may have been* underreported," said the form letters that went to mom-and-pop outfits all over the country. In its quest to close what it calls the tax gap—the difference between what Americans owe and what they pay—the IRS is using new and questionable tactics to uncover what it says are hundreds of billions of dollars in unpaid taxes each year. Mining databases of detailed credit card and debit card transactions, the service scours records to identify companies whose sales receipts fall outside normal patterns. This is the sort of thing marketers do every day to find potential customers, but it is a poor substitute for the level of proof that should be required to determine whether a business or individual is paying the right amount of taxes. In short, it's nothing more than a fishing expedition and an exercise that puts a heavy burden on mom-and-pop businesses, which are required to prove a negative: that they *didn't* underreport income. It's this kind of behavior that is making more and more Americans wonder whether the IRS has gone off the rails.

No federal agency strikes more fear into the hearts of Americans than the Internal Revenue Service, and for good reason. The IRS has the power to garnish your wages or seize your property for nonpayment, and unlike other creditors, it doesn't have to go to court to obtain a judgment against you to do so. When it comes to adjudicating tax claims, the IRS is both judge and jury. With its extensive power, you'd expect the agency to be judicious in its actions, but in recent years the opposite has been true. Even as it enforces a complex and confusing array of tax laws, internally it operates as anything but a watchful sentry for the nation's treasury. Top officials have allowed unrestrained spending for questionable uses. Units within the service have gone rogue, pursuing political agendas of their own. Fraud artists, sensing opportunity, have targeted the agency with scams to lighten taxpayers' wallets. On top of all this, the White House has settled more responsibilities on the agency's narrow shoulders. It's a recipe for disaster, not one to encourage the confidence of taxpayers. Let me show you how to handle this prickly pear and protect your wealth at the same time.

If there is one number among the many you need to remember when you think about the IRS, it's this: 4 million. That's the number of words in the tax code. That's longer than the Bible and longer than the Declaration of Independence, the Constitution, and the Gettysburg Address all put together! Reading and understanding the code is virtually impossible unless you are a highly trained tax professional. The language Congress has used to write the code is arcane and obtuse. To an outsider, it seems that Uncle Sam doesn't want people to understand the code, and for that reason, we spend more time and money every year complying with these byzantine rules. Americans spend an average of 15 hours completing their tax filings, of which 8 hours is for record keeping, 2 for tax planning, and 5 for form completion and submission. The average cost is $260.

Unfortunately, many Americans look at calls for simplification of the tax code as a shibboleth of the Right. In fact, the most trained and knowledgeable tax authorities say a simpler code should be a national priority. "The complexity of the tax code as it stands today is overwhelming, making compliance difficult for taxpayers and enforcement difficult for the IRS," says Nina Olson, who runs a special office advocating for taxpayers at the IRS. "With a simpler tax code, taxpayers would not need as much help complying, and the IRS could deliver on its revenue-collection mission with a smaller budget." Yet the IRS has virtually given up on its mission to help taxpayers understand what they owe. The agency was on track to answer less than half the calls to its information phone lines in 2015, the worst performance it has recorded since 2001. Nearly 9 million callers were disconnected by the IRS, a phenomenon the tax service calls "courtesy disconnects." Some courtesy! Hold times for taxpayers who did manage to get their calls answered stretched to 30 minutes, up from just 4 minutes in 2005. Even professionals said getting through to an IRS representative was virtually impossible and reported hold times of up to six hours. One tax pro I know said he combated the problem by getting into the office early, calling the help line, and working on returns while he waited for someone to pick up, usually at the end of the day. The IRS is printing and distributing fewer tax forms and explanatory pamphlets. Tax preparation that once was offered by satellite offices is a thing of the past.

All this adds up to an IRS that is ignoring its core mission of serving taxpayers. Instead, the agency is more focused on enforcement and closing the tax gap as a way of dealing with a shrinking budget. But this strategy is perilous for both taxpayers and tax collection. Currently, 98 percent of all tax collections are voluntary, and Olson maintains that boosting voluntary tax collections by distributing more information and answering more questions would result in higher tax collections than would conducting fishing expeditions such as the small-business enforcement effort I just described. Think of it this way: if the IRS collected 10 percent less in enforcement revenue, tax revenue would decline by less than $6 billion. If voluntary tax payments dropped by 10 percent, tax revenue would decline by more than $300 billion. Helping the vast majority of Americans pay their taxes would help both taxpayers and tax collections, but the agency has had other preoccupations.

The most astonishing of these is the outright abuse of the IRS's extensive powers. Beginning in March 2010, the IRS delayed or held up indefinitely applications by conservative groups for nonprofit status with words or phrases such as *Tea Party* and *Patriot* in their names. By withholding approval, the tax agency essentially stopped these groups from operating and silenced conservative voices. It's exactly as Supreme Court Justice John Marshall said in 1819: "The power to tax is the power to destroy." After its review, the General Accounting Office concluded that oversight at the IRS was so lax that it made it more likely that these conservative groups were targeted for audits. These abuses started with employees in the Cincinnati office of the IRS, who were tasked with reviewing applications by nonprofit organizations for tax-exempt status. IRS employees developed a "Be on the Lookout" (BOLO) spreadsheet of candidates that required extra scrutiny, including names related to the Tea Party movement. The practice of slowing reviews spread from Cincinnati to other IRS offices, including Laguna Niguel, California, and Washington, D.C. The IRS, by the way, is still refusing to release these BOLO lists, citing privacy concerns.

This hyperscrutiny of tax-exempt applications from conservative groups coincided with the Obama administration's political attacks on conservative donors such as the Koch brothers. One telling example is that of Media Trackers, a conservative organization that applied to the IRS for recognition of tax-exempt status and received no response after waiting 16 months. When the organization's founder, Drew Ryun, applied for tax-exempt status for an organization with the liberal-sounding name Greenhouse Solutions, that application was approved in three weeks. This would be funny if it weren't so tragic. Ryun is a former Republican Party staffer.

However, the brunt of the IRS's scrutiny was endured not by members of the media or their critics but by Americans who had been inspired by the Tea Party movement and wanted to get involved. Most chilling is the story of Catherine Engelbrecht, who says the application for tax-exempt status for her organization, True the Vote, which seeks to prevent voter fraud, was delayed for three years. The IRS asked her hundreds of questions, requesting every Facebook post and Twitter tweet she had ever written as well as information about her family, what organizations she had belonged to, and whether she had ever sought office. But that was just the beginning. What started as a lengthy and probing investigation into True the Vote by the IRS became a witch hunt. The Bureau of Alcohol, Tobacco, Firearms and Explosives audited the machine shop owned by Engelbrecht and her husband even though it doesn't make firearms. Next, the Occupational Safety and Health Administration inspected the shop, levying a $25,000 fine despite the fact that the inspector congratulated them on how tightly their operation was run. The FBI also came calling, probing for details about attendees at meetings of another political group Engelbrecht had founded. Daniel Henninger, an editor for the *Wall Street Journal*'s editorial page, wrote: "The IRS tea-party audit story isn't Watergate, it's worse than Watergate. . . . The Watergate break-in was the professionals of the party in power going after the party professionals of the party out of power. The IRS scandal is the party in power going after the most average Americans imaginable."

Although the scandal was viewed largely as a partisan debate by the mainstream media, the truth is that it was an astonishing misuse of government power. Despite the president's protestations that there wasn't a "smidgeon of corruption" at the IRS, the agency eventually had to admit its overreach after the inspector general for the Treasury Department released a report saying the agency had in fact targeted certain nonprofit groups for extra scrutiny. As always in American politics, it's the cover-up that proves to be the downfall of those in power. In spring 2015, the

Treasury Department's inspector general for tax administration found that the e-mails in question from the IRS regarding the scandal that its *own commissioner* had said had been lost and were irretrievable were in fact still sitting on the same backup tapes on which they had always been. IRS employees simply hadn't requested them. In other words, congressional investigators had been denied information that had been in plain view by an IRS unwilling to cooperate. It was that move which turned the IRS investigation into a criminal probe that took years to resolve. Is it any wonder that the left-leaning ACLU and others bristled when it was learned that the tax agency reserved for itself the power to read individual e-mails and other electronic communication *without* a subpoena?

The IRS's problems aren't limited to the exempt organizations unit. In fact, a variety of recent scandals point to an agency that is both arrogant and unrestrained in its use of taxpayer dollars. The agency spent $49 million between 2010 and 2012 to send employees to elaborate conferences all over the country. The most elaborate was a three-day junket to Anaheim, California, in 2010 called Leading into the Future. The event was worthy of a Wall Street clientele. IRS managers were greeted with a wine reception and free gifts such as briefcases. Many luxuriated in two-bedroom presidential suites. A speaker was paid $27,000 to pontificate on "radical innovation." A total of 15 outside speakers made presentations at a cost of $135,350. Planning the event cost the government a pretty penny. Three independent event planners were hired to find hotels and plan the proceedings at a cost of $133,000. More than 25 employees were sent on scouting trips to Anaheim at a cost of $36,000. Training videos prepared for the conference cost $50,000. One was a *Star Trek* parody that showed IRS employees discussing ways of finding tax fraud. Other conferences were held in luxury resorts in Las Vegas, where IRS workers stayed at the Caesar's Palace hotel and conference center, Mandalay Bay, and New York–New York Hotel & Casino. That's not the only financial abuse at the agency responsible for collecting our tax dollars. Another government watchdog report flagged misuse of government credit cards by IRS employees. More than 5,000 IRS card accounts racked up $103 million in purchases, some of them for wine and online pornography, between 2010 and 2011. IRS chieftains ignored Obama administration directives to cancel $70 million in discretionary employee bonuses when automatic spending cuts were in place in 2013. When the tax administrator handed out bonuses totaling $2.8 million to employees with disciplinary issues in 2014, including more than $1 million to workers who didn't pay their taxes, it barely lifted an eyebrow inside the Beltway. Three million dollars? That's pocket change. But it's this lack of concern about the dollars and cents of taxpayers that shows just how far the IRS has strayed from its mission as the nation's top tax collector. Clearly, the internal culture of the IRS is at odds with its mission, yet IRS commissioner John Koskinen blames tax cuts for what he admits is "crummy taxpayer service."

The tax agency's myriad problems are making it easy pickings for fraud artists. In recent years, emboldened scammers have found ways to steal tax refunds from taxpayers. Some breach the private accounts of tax software users, stealing account passwords to steal refunds. Others hack the IRS website itself. Some 100,000 accounts of U.S. taxpayers were hacked through the IRS website's "Get Transcript" function. Using information gleaned from other sources, the scammers correctly answered personal identity verification questions. In return, the thieves got the actual tax filings, including names and Social Security numbers, of filers and their children—a treasure trove of personal data. Taxpayers don't realize there is a problem until they file their taxes and the IRS tells them their refund check has already been sent—to someone else! The number of suspicious returns filed is growing rapidly. In 2012 the number was 2.5 million, up from 900,000 in 2010. Whistle-blowers say software providers may be inadvertently giving criminals cover, but it's clear the IRS isn't doing enough to flag fraudulent returns. Another scam involves fake IRS agents harassing taxpayers with threatening phone calls. The bad guys demand payment and threaten jail time if the victims don't send money. And they do. Some 366,000 people have paid $15.5 million to scammers over the last two years. It's hard to imagine that these scams could continue if the IRS was playing at the top of its game. But instead of reacting quickly, the agency's efforts are minimal.

It seems strange indeed that an agency that can barely manage to execute its core mission has been given a huge new responsibility at the president's direction. Under this administration, the agency has received vast new powers to interpret and enforce Obamacare. The law generated 47 major changes to the tax code, the most sweeping changes to tax law in 20 years. The responsibility for tracking the details of who has coverage and who does not has fallen to IRS agents. That means the agency will be responsible for determining who gets insurance subsidies and who does not, whether your coverage meets the requirements of Obamacare or whether it does not. The IRS will police the individual mandate and determine whether the coverage offered by private companies meets the rigorous requirements of the healthcare law. In short, the tax agency has expanded its mandate beyond tax collection to the interpretation and implementation of social policy. Early reports regarding the IRS's capacity for handling this vast responsibility were poor. Confusion reigned among Obamacare subsidy recipients. As many as half of the 6.8 million first-year recipients of Obamacare received subsidies that were too large as a result of a glitch at Healthcare.gov, wiping out highly anticipated tax refunds for many of them. Things were so disorganized and baffling that the government delayed refunds altogether for tens of thousands of Obamacare recipients. It was a disappointing showing for the tax agency and another reason the nation's tax collection authority has lost respect.

The problem for conservatives isn't simply how the IRS is doing its job; the tax law itself is infuriating. President Obama repeatedly and in many contexts has said that the rich should pay their "fair share" in taxes, but a recent study from the independent Congressional Budget Office (CBO) shows that the wealthy paid their fair share *and more* even before Obama imposed tax hikes targeting the well-to-do. The analysis takes as its starting point the idea that all income should be considered in interpreting tax payments across income lines. That means that Social Security, Medicare, and unemployment insurance payments are added into the equation as well as business income and income from capital gains. That broader reach reveals a highly unequal system of taxation, not one that shows that the wealthy aren't contributing. In fact, the CBO study shows that the bottom three-fifths of Americans (by income), or *60 percent* of all households in this country, are net recipients of government payments. In other words, they get more money in transfer payments from government programs than they pay in federal taxes. Those in the second-highest income quintile pay just slightly more in federal taxes ($14,800) than they receive in government transfer payments ($14,100), for a difference of just $700 a year. The vast preponderance of tax payments is made by the top one-fifth of U.S. households by income. In fact, the top 20 percent of American households in terms of income finance 100 percent of the transfer payments to the bottom 60 percent and nearly all the tax revenue collected to run the federal government.

These facts point out that the president's rhetoric regarding the 1 percent is just that: rhetoric or political speech. Likewise, his idea that soaking the rich can fill tax coffers simply doesn't work. Consider Britain. After Prime Minister Gordon Brown's government announced a plan to levy a 50 percent income tax on people earning 1 million pounds or more, the number of folks in that category shrank. The number of millionaire tax filers in Britain in 2009 was 16,000. By 2010, that number had dropped to 6,000. The government had pinned its hopes on raising 2.5 billion pounds in new revenue, but the law of unintended consequences took hold. Before the law changed in 2009–2010, British millionaires contributed 13.5 billion pounds, or 9 percent of the total tax liability paid by taxpayers. After the change in the tax law, millionaires contributed 6.5 billion pounds, or less than 4.5 percent of the total tax liability. To be sure, some of the well to do in Britain might have become thousandaires in the Great Recession that started in the United States, but another reason for the strange disappearance of England's well heeled is that people in this class don't necessarily stay put when things turn against them. Like Gérard Depardieu in France, some pull up stakes and move to a more welcoming spot. In short, raising tax requirements doesn't mean that increased tax revenue follows.

Even so, the president continues to propose changes that would burden those who guide their own ships. Obamacare alone has 20 new taxes. The president has increased capital gains taxes twice and proposed raising them yet again in January 2015. Then there is his death tax proposal. President Obama has proposed changes to inheritance and capital gains taxes that would raise the estate tax to the highest levels in the industrial world. The plan would eliminate what accountants call the step-up basis at death on capital gains taxation, raising the top capital gains tax rate to 28 percent from 20 percent. Under current law, when a parent or a grandparent dies, the increase in value of his or her assets is not taxed as income (because the inheritor will pay estate tax). But the president's plan would tax estates and impose the regular capital gains tax on inherited assets, whether business, property, or stocks, bringing the effective death tax rate to 57 percent. That's two taxes where one existed before. The administration says its intention is to close a tax loophole, but the impact of such a move if it became law would effectively prevent family businesses from being passed between generations. Conservatives think of estate taxes as wrong on their face. Remember, estate taxes are levied on money that already has been taxed!

I'd like to write that we've come a long way on the nation's fiscal policy in the last six years, but the opposite is true. The president's mind seemed open to change when in 2010 he appointed a bipartisan National Commission on Fiscal Responsibility and Reform piloted by two people who had spent many years studying the topic, Erskine Bowles and Alan Simpson. They were charged with proposing recommendations to balance the budget and address the rapid-fire growth of entitlement spending and the gap between revenues and spending by the federal government. The group met and produced a very nice bound report full of sane solutions, but nothing happened as a result of those recommendations. Instead, five years later, the administration began to consider the possibility of using executive orders to raise taxes. It started with a trial balloon floated by Vermont senator Bernie Sanders, who called on the president to raise more than $100 billion in taxes through executive action. Instead of batting away the suggestion as undemocratic, the president's aides declared that Obama was "very interested" in the idea. In the short span of five years, the president had moved 180 degrees, from attempting to find solutions to our nation's fiscal crisis by consensus to getting the money for his pet programs on his own and ignoring the directive of the Constitution that "all Bills for raising Revenue shall originate in the House of Representatives." Shocking!

PAYING ONLY WHAT YOU OWE

Since the IRS has shown itself not to be an advocate for taxpayers and is burdening us with new responsibilities, it's up to you to protect your wealth. Your goal is to preserve as much of your wealth as possible to pass it along to your family. Nothing I advocate here is contrary to tax law. That would be stupid and could end up costing you more than you save in back taxes and penalties. The idea is to stay within the law and take advantage of the benefits that the law offers to shelter income and pass it on to the next generation. Tax law rewards certain behaviors, such as buying a home and saving in a 401(k) or IRA. Taking advantage of these offerings requires planning and strict attention to detail, especially saving and cataloging records. The time-tested methods for managing your tax burden include shifting income and deductions to the tax years that will result in lowest taxes, maximizing tax-free sources of income (a topic we explored in Chapter 5), and exploiting every single deduction you can find.

HIRING A PRO

Tax fraud, especially the sort in which crooks steal the refunds of unsuspecting tax filers, has gone through the roof. The bad guys have been stealing refunds for years by surreptitiously getting Social Security numbers and filing returns under those numbers. But these days they've gone one better. Some are finding ways to steal the passwords that tax filers use to set up accounts to file their taxes by using

popular tax software packages. The impact is the same: the bad guys steal the victims' refunds. One accountant told me that a client of his was due tens of thousands from the government the year Superstorm Sandy demolished his house. The man desperately needed that refund, but a crook had stolen it before he filed his taxes. Fixing that problem, my accountant friend said, had taken literally years of IRS badgering and filling out forms. According to some state tax authorities, online tax fraud by thieves using legitimate tax software is up 37 percent. The incidence of fraud was so common that Intuit, the maker of the nation's most popular tax software, TurboTax, temporarily suspended the transmission of e-filed state tax returns early in the 2014 tax filing season.

Protecting yourself isn't easy, but hiring a responsible tax professional will at least give you an ally if the worst happens. Truth is, tax professionals also use tax software and file electronically, but if you fall victim to tax fraud, at least you'll have someone to argue your case. And let's face it, having a tax professional at your side makes all the sense in the world in light of the complexity of the tax code. For my money, the only reason not to have a professional is that you are in a first job. There's nothing like doing your own taxes to learn firsthand the basics of how the tax system works. But for most of us there are plenty of reasons to hire a tax pro. It's best to use a professional when you own your own business, you've gone through a major life change such as marriage or divorce, you've bought or sold a home in the previous year,

you own rental property, or you have a large investment port-folio. In other words, if your finances are complicated for any reason, it pays to hire a professional. If you manage to pick an experienced accountant, you'll find that he or she probably has prepared a return for someone in your exact situation or a very similar one. What's more, if the IRS has issues with the filing, such as wanting more information, your professional will handle the exchange.

Finding the right tax pro is a whole other kettle of fish. If you pick a tax preparer the IRS considers a cheat or incompetent, the chances of getting audited go through the roof. Every IRS district manager knows the problem tax filers in his or her district. Consider a man I met several years ago who was driving home from work one wintry night listening to the radio and heard a report of a man who had fallen 100 feet to his death in a river. The man wasn't surprised to find out that the suicide was his accountant, who had pushed questionable tax strategies. The man I met was audited by the IRS for tax filings going back three years and ended up with a $5,000 bill in back taxes and penalties. He wasn't the only one. The accountant left a long trail of troubles.

Okay, most people's accountants don't fling themselves to their death, but screwups are commonplace. Some are innocent, such as transposing numbers or forgetting a signature, but others are more serious, such as the ones committed by the wintry weather suicide, who once had suggested to a client that he claim more dependents than he actually

had. You won't get much help from trade groups or even the IRS in trying to make sure the tax professional you pick is on the up and up, and so some due diligence is essential. Check out your state board of accountancy to make sure any CPA you use is licensed and doesn't have any disciplinary actions against him or her. You can get contact information at NASBA.org. Interview anyone you consider working with face-to-face and ask the tough questions, such as how many of his or her clients have been audited and whether he or she has ever been audited. It's critical that you pick a pro whom you can trust and can work with for years to come. A qualified individual won't just fill out the tax form for you but also give you advice on how to position your assets for the long term to result in the lowest possible tax bill. Unfortunately, there are many varieties of people who put themselves out as tax professionals. Sorting them out isn't easy.

Certified public accountants are the gold standard, having completed a four-part accounting exam, and they can represent you in front of the IRS if it ever comes to that. However, there are less expensive ways to get help. Enrolled agents who have passed a tax exam may have worked at the IRS and are licensed to file taxes. You can find an enrolled agent at www.naea.org. Some Certified Financial Planners (CFPs) also offer tax services. At a minimum, you want your CFP to be talking to whoever prepares your taxes. Another option is to use accredited tax accountants and tax-planning services. (I did say it was a whole other kettle of fish, right?)

Getting a preparer who is recommended by someone you know and trust is good idea, too.

If you do plan to use tax software, make sure your password is strong to protect yourself from the fraudsters. The good news is that the software does all the math for you, making every calculation. The way the packages work is that they have you fill out the forms by asking you questions and prompting you for responses. For some of us, it comes down to comfort level. Do you want to handle your taxes on your own, or do you want a pro to do it for you? Either way you file, your return will go to the IRS electronically, and that will guarantee the quickest processing.

TAKING ALL THE DEDUCTIONS YOU ARE DUE

My advice is to leave no stone unturned when it comes to deductions. People write entire books about the thousands of obscure deductions that the tax code allows, and even the IRS expects you to take full advantage of all the deductions you can find to save on your tax bill. You'll have to itemize your taxes and fill out the long form to claim them, but the benefits can be huge. In 2012, 97 million taxpayers claimed $1.18 trillion in write-offs. You can share in the wealth. Here are a handful of overlooked deductions that can bring your tax bill down. **College loan interest** is a critical deduction for parents and their children struggling with the high cost of education. You can deduct up to $2,500 of annual interest on loans to pay for college. Income phaseouts exist, naturally, and so high earners might want to consider taking out a home equity loan instead, which in most cases will allow you to deduct interest. For more on how to juggle college debt and deductions, check out Chapter 3. **Private mortgage insurance.** You already have learned all about the home mortgage interest deduction, and although that deduction is now on a phaseout schedule for high earners, others may benefit from it. PMI is an insurance policy that lenders require if you can't make a 20 percent down payment on a home. This is a break that Congress reviews every year, and it will expire for 2015 unless Congress renews it. Make sure it has been renewed before claiming it. You'll find the amount of PMI you paid on your bank's Mortgage Interest Statement, Form 1098. The break is available to home owners who took out a mortgage after January 1, 2007. Like a lot of deductions, this one has income phaseouts. The sweet spot for this break is an adjusted gross income below $109,000. **Caring for a dependent parent** can save you money on taxes if you can claim a parent as a dependent. Your parent or parents must live with you and get more than half of their support from you. Keep in mind that the parent's earnings must be less than the tax exemption level. The devil is in the details with this one, and you should consult a tax professional. But if you meet the requirements, you'll be able to claim an added personal exemption on your income tax return. Another plus is that any medical expenses you pay for that parent can contribute to the threshold for deducting medical costs. To meet that threshold, you have to spend 10 percent or more of your adjusted gross income on medical expenses. If you or your spouse is age 65 or older, the 7.5 percent threshold is maintained through 2016. **Home equity loan interest** is deductible on loans of up to $100,000 no matter what you do with the money, as is, of course, qualified **mortgage interest** paid on up to $1 million of loans to purchase or improve your primary and secondary residence. (Again, phaseouts occur at higher income levels.) **Job search** expenditures are also deductible. If you were looking for a job last year, even if you were unsuccessful, those costs can be deducted as miscellaneous expenses. If you do land a new gig, you also can claim relocation expenses for a new job. A tax professional can help you with details. You also can write off **worthless securities.** Just keep in mind that the stocks, bonds, or notes you write off must be completely without value. You can look as far back as seven years to find investments that fit the bill. Don't forget to write off any professional fees related to filing your taxes, securing alimony, or planning your estate.

There are many more deductions, but you should be aware that some of them are IRS audit bait. Deductions that may get a second look from the tax agency include home office deductions, which draw attention, especially if you claim a salaried income. Noncash charitable donations also are scrutinized, particularly if you contribute a car or another large noncash item. But even large cash contributions to charity can draw attention.

When it comes to deductions, one of the things IRS auditors keep in mind is how you stack up against other taxpayers. CCH calculated average deductions, and although you shouldn't use them as a hard and fast guide to your own tax return, it makes sense to have a general idea of what people in your income bracket claim as deductions. For example, folks with an income range of $50,000 to $100,000 on average claim medical expenses of $7,312, interest of $9,320, and charitable contributions of $2,815. Claiming deductions far larger than the average in your income range may result in more scrutiny of your 1040 by the IRS because much of the heavy lifting of finding audit candidates is computerized.

BEING AWARE OF THE
ALTERNATIVE MINIMUM TAX

A s if the tax system weren't enough of a burden, there is another tax system. The dreaded alternative minimum tax (AMT) is a second tax regime operated by the IRS that Congress set up to catch wealthy tax cheats way back in 1969. The idea is to get you to pay more under AMT, and to this day this alternative system is still boosting tax bills for Americans. Although the original AMT system ensnared only 19,000 people, in later years millions were forced to pay

AMT, as brackets and exemptions were never indexed for inflation. Here's how AMT works. Under regular IRS rules, you calculate your federal taxes, starting with gross income, and then subtract deductions. Under AMT, you start with gross income, but you can't use many of the deductions you may be accustomed to. Key breaks such as the deductions for state and local income tax, property tax, and home equity loan interest disappear. Exemptions for children are gone. Even though the highest tax rate under AMT of 28 percent is lower than the highest rate under the regular tax system of 39.6 percent, people pay more in taxes under AMT because of the loss of these deductions. That's the reason so many people fear the AMT. Fortunately, the American Taxpayer Relief Act of 2012 permanently patched the inflation issue, but AMT is still a threat to ordinary taxpayers, particularly in high-tax states that result in bigger tax deductions. Those who are likely to get caught in the crosshairs are people with high family income, generally $250,000 and higher; large state and local income and property taxes to deduct; and a spouse and several children. Large home equity mortgage interest also can play a role. In short, the more deductions you tend to take, the more likely you are to end up owing AMT, up to a point. At high earner levels of $750,000 and more, tax rates of 39.6 percent probably will result in higher tax payments without the AMT. But the sweet spot for capturing Americans in the AMT tax system is upper middle income with high deductions. A decent accountant will run your taxes both under AMT rules and under the regular system to make sure you don't fall under AMT. The best-case scenario is that you run a mock calculation before the end of the year so that you can determine whether making a few adjustments to your gross income, such as making a contribution to your IRA, prepaying deductible business expenses, or selling losing investments in a taxable broker-age account, can keep you out of the clutches of the AMT.

THE BEST TIME TO PLAN IS THE YEAR BEFORE

The best time to lower your tax bill is the December *before* you file. Truth is, once you pop the champagne bottle, scream "Happy New Year," and give your significant other a kiss at midnight, almost all of your tax-planning strategies are lost if you haven't already implemented them. Before the end of the year, consider these strategies:

SELL YOUR LOSERS. If you invest in individual stocks out-side a retirement plan and have enjoyed gains, analyze your portfolio to identify any losers you have. If you sell those los-ers, you can use the capital losses to offset your capital gains, plus you can take an additional $3,000 in losses against your other income. You can buy back those losers next year if you plan to hold them for the long term. Avoid tripping IRS wash-sale rules by buying back the same securities no less than 30 days after you sold them.

DELAY TAKING YOUR BONUS. One easy way to reduce your income is to get your boss to delay giving you your year-end bonus until after the first of the next year. That way your bonus won't show up as income in the current tax year. If you are self-employed, delay invoices until after the first of the year.

SET ASIDE MORE FOR RETIREMENT. Most people don't contribute the maximum they are eligible for to their workplace retirement fund. According to the IRS, contribution limits are $17,500 for 2014 and $18,000 for 2015. Catch-up limits for workers age 50 and older are $5,500 for 2014 and $6,000 for 2015. Check the rules for contributing to your 401(k) to make sure you can modify contributions at any time. Remember, the money you contribute to your 401(k) or an IRA comes out before you pay taxes (as long as you are within the contribution limits). Why not pay yourself before paying Uncle Sam?

GIVE TO CHARITY. If you are already planning to give money to your favorite charity, this is the time to do it. In addition to cash, you can give household goods, clothing, and even a car. But before you send that old junker off, talk to a tax professional to make sure you are doing it the right way. Vehicle contributions often are scrutinized by the IRS.

PAY YOUR TUITION BILL EARLY. If you've got a child in college, your spring semester bill isn't likely to be due until January, but it may be worthwhile to pay it now. Early payers can claim the American Opportunity Tax Credit on their current-year returns. The credit is worth up to $2,500 and up to 40 percent of it is refundable, which means you could get back as much as $1,000 as a tax refund if you don't owe taxes. You can claim tuition, fees, and course materials.

Finally, don't leave any money on the table. Be sure to use any money you've set aside in your flexible spending account at work. Like a 401(k), FSA money goes into the account before taxes, but if you fail to use that money in the same year in which it is contributed, you could lose it.

AVOIDING AN AUDIT

The more you make, the more likely you are to get audited. Taxpayers earning $200,000 or more have an audit rate three times higher than that of the general population, and if you're earning a million dollars, your chances jump to one in nine. Even if you aren't in those brackets, you can find yourself face to face with an IRS audit. One way to escape the IRS's notice is to fit in with the pack. I mentioned before that you want to keep your deductions near levels that Americans in your tax bracket claim, and there is a really good reason for that. The IRS conducts roboaudits, relying on automation and computer programs to flag returns that are out of step with the majority. Other items can get you a second look. If you submit a sloppy return with typos and bad math, watch out. One common reason people get audited is that the information they input into their forms is different from the information on their W-2s or 1099s. Double-check all your numbers and income sources when you file. Also, claim any new dependents on just one tax form. Claiming dependents who are claimed by someone else or have already filed a return and claimed themselves is a no-no. This is a big red flag to the IRS. I have mentioned that high-income filers attract attention, but so do people who claim to have zero income, especially people who run their own businesses. Don't even consider setting up an unprofitable business just to reap the tax breaks. And for goodness' sake, don't forget to claim income. If you get income from various sources, you'll need to report it even if a 1099 doesn't reach your mailbox because the employer no doubt will report your pay to the IRS on its income tax form. It's easy to lose track of these payments over the course of the year. Keep good records.

Finally, if the worst happens and you are contacted by the IRS, don't panic. The IRS sends out millions of what it calls Automated Correspondence Exam notices each year that are generated by computer algorithms that catch something unusual. The best response is quick and accurate information to set the record straight.

MY LAST WORD ON TAXES

People often ask me how far they can go in claiming deductions such as unreimbursed employee business expenses. What happens if they forget to report a small source of income? Can they push the line, shade the truth, and get away with it? To be sure, in recent years the IRS has been down on its heels, preoccupied with scandal and burdened with additional responsibilities. But you couldn't be more wrong in thinking this is the time to save a few dollars by cheating because the IRS in future years can go back and scrutinize previous tax year returns. According to its website, in extreme cases the IRS will look back at as many as six years of returns for errors. My advice is to stay within the law but exploit every advantage you can legally take.

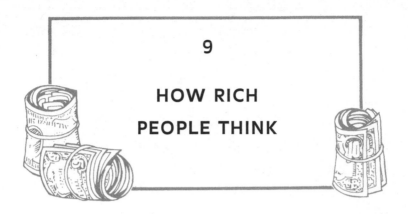

9

HOW RICH
PEOPLE THINK

The neighborhood where I spent most of my growing-up years was strictly middle class. We lived in a brick home on a half-acre lot in a suburb of Cincinnati, Ohio. There was no golf club membership or swimming pool membership. For entertainment in the summer, we watched the Cincinnati Reds annihilate nearly every team it played, or at least it seemed that way to me. By getting straight A's on my report card, I earned free tickets for our family, a contribution that made me beam with pride. If we weren't attending a game, we listened on radio, and even today listening to baseball on a warm summer night makes me smile. My growing-up years were a happy time but not a wealthy time.

My constant companion back then was a neighbor named Debbie. I spent hours at her house playing with Barbie dolls and eating French fries her mother would make for us in a deep fryer. Her father groomed their yard with care, and the house was a neighborhood showplace for its landscaping. The cars in their driveway were American, and they never took extravagant vacations. What I didn't know was that Debbie's family was on its way to becoming wealthy. Her father, an electrician with his own business, made a decent living, but he and his wife managed their finances with care. They became millionaires in an era when being a millionaire really meant something. If you saw him in his yard in white T-shirt and jeans, you would have guessed he was living paycheck to paycheck and working a blue-collar job. But the truth was far different. He paid for all three of his children to go to college—in cash—and retired comfortably. He was a huge success but was never flashy.

Public policies of the last six years haven't favored individuals who want to be financially independent and successful in their own right, but people are still, like Debbie's father, getting ahead. In this final chapter, I want to look at the characteristics of people who've managed to go against the tide and achieve financial success on their own terms.

Attitude is the key. If you want to achieve any goal, you have to have the right frame of mind. I believe the critical ingredient in becoming financially successful is believing it can happen. America continues to hold great prospects for those who want to accumulate wealth. Those benefits flow to people who understand that our nation's economy and social system are fluid. I see too many Americans, particularly young people, who believe that the modest background they are from is where they will stay. They think that only wealthy families produce financially successful offspring. The rich are born with silver spoons in their mouths, they believe. In this way, President Obama's rhetoric about the 1 percent of Americans controlling the nation's wealth has done much harm. More and more people buy the idea that the fix is in and only the government can save them from financial distress. This attitude could not be more wrong. When Thomas Stanley and William Danko wrote their groundbreaking book *The Millionaire Next Door*, they found through extensive research that more than half of the nation's millionaires had not received a single dollar in inheritance money. They were first-generation wealthy. So much for silver spoons! Hard work and planning, I believe, makes the difference for American families who achieve financial success.

The financially successful also have other critical attitudes. They feel they are responsible for their own future and take that responsibility seriously. They don't worship money but respect it. These are people who don't pay full price for anything. Money is a tool to the ends they want to achieve, not the goal in its own right. Consider my friend Jonathan. He worked as a kitchen porter years ago at a fashionable New York restaurant but spent his free time at the library reading financial publications. Friends at work said he'd come into the kitchen with the *Wall Street Journal* under his arm. He was determined to succeed after a tortured childhood in which he faced multiple illnesses and was branded a failure at school. "Most of the restaurant staff would go drinking," he recalls. "I'd go home and study and sleep. They made the decision to spend, and I'd made the decision to save and invest. Multiply that by 365 days, throw in a little investment success, and at the end of the year, one guy's got $20,000 and everyone else is penniless. Multiply and compound that by 10 years, and one guy is home and dry and all the others are going to be waiting tables for the rest of their lives." Today Chris is retired at age 55 and enjoying his life. It was Chris's ability to work and his desire to make it on his own that led to his success.

Another trait I see over and over again among the financially successful is that they are resilient. If fate throws them a curve, they don't look for someone to blame; they get up and try again. Babe Ruth was one of the greatest baseball players who ever lived. He hit 714 home runs over his career, but he struck out nearly twice as often. Even the greats have to deal with failure. It comes with the territory. The same is true for managing your own money and becoming financially successful. Peter Lynch, the legendary Fidelity Magellan portfolio manager who advised small investors to "buy what you know," could boast annual returns of an astonishing 29 percent, yet even he said that picking winners was not easy. "In this business, if you're good, you are right six times out of ten. You're never going to be right nine times out of ten."

In Chapter 5, I described my philosophy of investing,

but there is much more to being financially successful than guiding your own retirement portfolio. Truth is, there are a handful of issues that set back families, even ones with fat portfolios. So many families overindulge their children day to day but fail to have a will that would pass on their savings if the worst happened. Debt, particularly the sort that comes from day-to-day overspending, can sap your best efforts to prepare for your future. Divorce is a huge financial negative for the families that endure it.

Financially successful Americans avoid debt. They know either intuitively or through experience the toll that having personal debt takes. Even a small credit card debt of $5,000, for example, can spiral out of control. At a monthly payment of $200 and an interest rate of 16.5 percent, the repayment period stretches out to 10 years and 9 months. Total interest paid will be more than half of the debt, or $2,510. I am not one of those people who believe that credit cards are the source of all consumer evils. In fact, they are powerful tools for people who use them correctly by not rolling debt month to month or using them only in the event of an emergency. But let's face it, that $2,500 in interest payments could be better used to start a child's college fund or as a down payment on a car. Debt is a waste of time and a burden you are better off without.

Successful Americans are generous with their gifts to children but don't jeopardize their own financial well-being to make their offspring happy. I see so many young parents who can't deny their children even the most frivolous consumer items, and those gifts can become habits on which children can become dependent. According to Pew Research, 48 percent of middle-aged adults with grown children gave them financial support. And for 27 percent of grown children, Mom and Dad were their primary source of income. There is no doubt kids are relying much more on their parents today than previous generations ever did. In fact, many have become so accustomed to support that they expect it. It's easy to understand why. The economy is failing to provide opportunities that would make it easier for grown children to stand on their own, and college loans are burdensome. Many families, though, are taking their assistance to an extreme. Tapping your retirement savings to help your child get a degree is a strategy bound to end badly. Again, nobody will lend you money for retirement. It makes no sense for your children to attend a pricey college where the dining hall serves made-to-order omelets while you eat Quaker Oats every morning to finance your child's lifestyle. One of the smartest things I see parents do is to set limits on spending. Since just 39 percent of college students graduate in four years, you can start by telling your children that if they want financial help from Mom and Dad, they better plan to finish their education on time.

Remember, not every college grad relies on the Bank of Their Parents. When Deena, a woman I interviewed not too long ago, discovered that her student loan debt would take her 10 years to pay off, she switched to a more lucrative job, got a roommate to share housing costs, and began paying more than her monthly student loan payments of $360. She wasn't earning a fortune—she made only $30,000—but she still was able to pay off the debt in three years by being disciplined and staying focused on her goals. Eradicating her student loan debt gave her the confidence to tackle new financial goals. "Once I became eligible for my company's 401(k), I paid in enough to get the match. Now I'll be boosting that contribution amount." There's a young woman who some day will be a millionaire!

Another thing that I see successful families do is stay together. It sounds simple, but divorce is a scourge that bankrupts millions of families. The statistics are astonishing. In the United States, there is one divorce approximately every 36 seconds. That's nearly 2,400 divorces per day, 16,800 per week, and 876,000 per year. Forty-one percent of first marriages end in divorce. And once you're divorced, your chances of getting divorced again rise dramatically. Sixty percent of second marriages and 73 percent of third marriages end in divorce. I was astonished not too long ago when my doctor told me the story of his own divorce, a million-dollar mess that took years out of his life and an untold emotional toll. This was a man who would have been hugely successful financially but for an acrimonious divorce.

His situation was unusual. After all, not every family goes through a high-profile court battle. Still, the cost of divorce decimates a family's wealth-building ability.

The bigger point here is the ongoing costs for a family that splits. Typically, costs for everything double. There are two payments for housing and two mortgages or, more likely, a mortgage and rent that still have to be paid. Child support, household expenses, utilities, groceries, and the like, double. Meanwhile, the same level of income has to suffice to cover this doubling of costs. There is no way to put a pretty face on this: divorce is expensive and can derail your financial future.

Being a success financially seems to come intuitively to some of us. Some people have the basic habits of mind and money that drive them to secure a stable future for their families. Many of these habits are good not just for your finances but also for your peace of mind. Keeping debt low also means that you won't stay up late at night worrying about the credit card bill. Telling your children what you expect out of them will keep them from becoming dependent on you.

The financially successful people I meet also have a clearly defined sense of values. They know what their goals are and work toward them every day. If what you want is a secure future for your family, you're less likely to throw away money on Manolo Blahniks. What's more, people who are on the right track understand that the game they are playing is a long-haul one. They are long-distance runners with the finish line in mind all the time. They know that achieving their goals will be a lifetime endeavor. For that reason, they can be flexible with the details. A friend of mine says that people who succeed at managing their money are more likely to view a problem as a challenge. If the roof caves in and requires $15,000 to fix, they are likely to view it as a problem that could happen to anyone and to work toward a solution rather than settle into fear. Typically, success of any sort requires good luck, but planning and hard work are what makes the difference.

In sum, it is true that it is harder these days to make it on your own and become a financial success. Poor government policies have made sure of that. But it still can be done. I have great confidence in the American people to overcome the burdens of high taxes and government bureaucracy to create lives of their own that are comfortable and full of abundance. And I firmly believe you can be part of that success story!

INDEX

Index

Index

Index